Praise for
Building the World's Great
Student Leader and I

"Park and Guy show us how to build a place where we are all valued and we all matter: It starts with building the understanding that each one of us has value, regardless of where we are in life."

--**Mike Smith Live**, Speaker, Professional Teenager

"Richard Parkhouse is a role model for educators and students alike: his life is built around service, compassion, and character. These ideals are what student leaders should strive for as they work toward becoming the best version of themselves, creating great high schools along the way."

--**Houston Kraft**, Student Leadership Trainer

"Park and Guy are legendary icons in celebrating student and staff success, spreading awareness of WE instead of me, and building positive school cultures across the nation."

--**Danny V. Batimana**, Happiness is NOW, Inc.

"Student leaders play a critical role in Building the World's Greatest High School because they are the role models, the initiators, and most of all the friends and peers of the students that walk the halls. Every student is looking for someone to pattern their life after, and how cool is it when students model service, compassion, and spirit and other students on campus want to be a part of what they are creating!! This book will guide the leaders at your school and as a result be a guide to every student on your campus."

--**Phil Boyte**, Author of *School Culture by Design*

Other Books by Park and Dr. Guy

Building the World's Greatest High School

Building the World's Greatest High School Workbook

Add Park on Snapchat

@parksgreatest
www.edalchemy.com

Add Dr. Guy on Snapchat

@guyewhite
www.guyewhite.com

BUILDING THE WORLD'S GREATEST HIGH SCHOOL STUDENT LEADER

RICHARD PARKHOUSE
& GUY E. WHITE, Ed.D.

BUILDING THE WORLD'S GREATEST HIGH SCHOOL STUDENT LEADER: CREATING A CULTURE OF SIGNIFICANCE WHERE EVERYONE MATTERS

RICHARD PARKHOUSE & GUY E. WHITE, ED.D.

PUBLISHED BY:

TRIUMPHANT HEART INTERNATIONAL, INC.
10117 SE SUNNYSIDE RD, F-403
HAPPY VALLEY, OR 97015

GET FREE TRAINING AT
WWW.WORLDSGREATESTHIGHSCHOOL.COM

LIBRARY OF CONGRESS CONTROL NUMBER: 2016932780

WGHSSL_B1_170816

DEDICATION

"In Honor of Our Teachers."

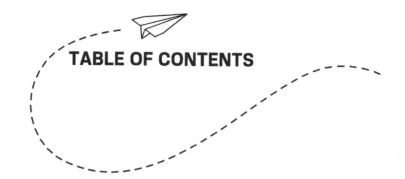

TABLE OF CONTENTS

NOTE FROM THE AUTHORS

"We greatly respect the people with which we serve and the sacredness of our work with students and educators. Accordingly, the names of certain people and places in this volume have been changed."

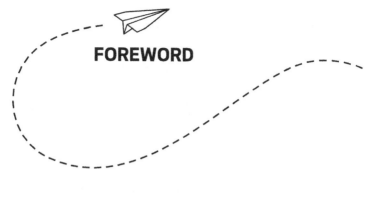

BECOMING MY WORLD'S GREATEST ME

With Keith Hawkins

Over twenty-two years, I have traveled across North America speaking to over 400,000 students, teachers, parents, and business leaders. Where I went to school, I was a typical student from a poverty-stricken environment. With hard work, a good attitude, and the willingness to follow great leaders, I turned my life around. Who would have ever thought that I would one day be considered a leader on my high school campus, let alone the president? The "World's Greatest Me" concept tells my story. It truly describes my belief and understanding of schools and that every person has what it takes to be the greatest person they can be.

I don't think I was any different than you or any other student in my school. I was a typical teenager who wanted to be accepted for who I truly was, and I wanted to feel like I belonged at the school. Not one student is raising their hand saying, "I want to be the loser." We all would like to feel like we matter, just the way we are. I really struggled with this because of my insecurities, and there were times where I felt like I lost my way. I started to follow just about anyone who would accept me. The problem was the person they were accepting wasn't the real me. It was a person wearing a mask to fit in. How do we get out from behind that mask and dare to show people who we truly are?

When I look at the six core values of the "World's Greatest High School," one of those values strikes a chord deep inside me. Growing up in a tough part of Los Angeles, in a single-parent home, being raised with my brother and sister, the future for us was one with no hope. If you got to school, you were considered successful. Being the best me was really never even a thought that crossed my mind. The culture of every school I attended was one of stress. Being stressed was more common than learning the classroom work. The stress that students brought into the school created a climate that was dim and hopeless. You could see it in the teachers' eyes. Any hope of teaching students was sucked right out of the teachers. Disciplining the students was more common than teaching. It was nearly impossible for any student to learn. When teachers stop caring and students feel hopeless, there is a culture of complacency and apathy. No student really felt like they had a future, so it seemed.

As a child, I remember coming home to an environment full of heartache. I never forgot my freshman year when I came home and the lights were out. My mom couldn't afford to pay the bill, and as a result, we didn't have lights for four months. I remember my mom taking me to a friend's house for a sleepover that ended up lasting two weeks. I remember the days of looking in the refrigerator or cabinets and finding no food. This circumstance was common for the students at my school. It made learning in school really difficult. Most of all, it was demoralizing. It was hard to have self-worth when everything around you seemed so worthless.

What the administrators and teachers failed to realize was that the focus should not have been on the students' issues outside the building. The focus needed to be on creating an environment and culture in the school where everyone could maximize their ability to become their best – an environment where students can connect to the things that should matter to the students. The helplessness that was felt by the students sprung from the lack of connection they felt with the school and the teachers. So many teachers make the mistake of only showing the students the "teacher" side of them instead of showing the students all of them. This creates a relationship that has no connection. In order to walk down the road of becoming the best you,

you have to find out what gives you purpose. My belief is when someone finds purpose, he or she becomes passionate! Once someone has purpose and passion, that's when he or she feels empowered. When people are empowered, they realize that nothing can stop them from becoming who they truly want to be in high school and beyond.

I will never forget the time that a student leader named Lucy reached out to me. I was so taken aback by the fact that she saw leadership potential in me. One day in the school quad, she walked out and approached me in front of all my friends. She asked me my name, and she seemed to care so much about what I thought about the school and what I could do personally to make the school better. This was shocking to me because, up to this point, I was always considered a bad student or an average student at best. This made me realize that maybe my situation did not dictate who I was: It was what I decided to do with my life that dictated what kind of future I would have. This is when I truly started to take steps in the right direction. The mask I had been wearing to cover my insecurities started to peel away. I started to realize I could choose who I was, no matter what my situation was.

When you talk about becoming the greatest person you can be, that process exploded for me during my high school years. Garey High School was the World's Greatest High School with the World's Greatest teachers. The reason why I became the "Greatest Me" was because those teachers and administrators gave me something to do, something to hope for, and something to love. Ultimately, this allowed me to be the "World's Greatest Me." I used to bring all my outside frustrations to school and take them out on other people. I thought that every student's life was better than mine, so I was jealous. I was doing something that you should never do. I was comparing. Whenever you compare yourself with another, someone ends up better or they end up less. In the game of comparing, there's always a winner and loser. For example, when you're in class and you compare yourself with other students, you start to think, "Who's smarter? Am I as smart as these other students?" You and your peers compare your homes, friends, people you date, siblings, clothes, body sizes, parents, etc. None of the results of the comparison are true. All this does is stop us from finding out what our true gifts are. It stops the potential of becoming the greatest you.

We never know the impact that we have on students and their day-to-day lives and their futures by taking our frustrations out on them. Most frustrations come from things we cannot control, and when we compare ourselves with our fellow classmates, it only makes things worse. During my sophomore year in school, comparing my family to others became a drag. I knew something had to change. I started to take my role as a leader seriously. I realized that every action we take has some type of impact on others. Up to that point, for so many years, the impact I had on other students was negative, but at the same time, I was still a leader. What I realized was that I wanted to have an impact on others, but I wanted the impact to be positive. What took me by surprise was when I reached out to my peers I learned that everyone had things in their life that caused frustration. I realized that everyone who gave the effort to come to school was doing their best and bringing their best. In fact, I could have a positive impact on them and their future. This became my gift. I could inspire and empower my fellow students to realize their full potential and how bright their future could be. When this was all said and done, helping others realize they had a gift made me realize that was my gift. Through this process I learned so much about other students and, in return, learned more about the person I wanted to be.

Unfortunately, there was a culture at our school where underclassmen were treated "less than." I remember this because of how badly my friends and I were treated as freshmen. My sophomore year, in the boy's locker room, I decided to make a stand. Some of the upperclassmen were picking on some freshmen, and I stood up. I'll never forget my friend, Myron, asking me, "Why do you care what we do to the freshmen?" I responded by saying, "I remember what it was like to be one of those freshmen, and it didn't feel good. As long as I'm at this school, I'm going to make sure that no freshman or anyone else feels bad about being who they are." I'm so thankful that I took that stand. Shortly after, the freshman students started to approach me with smiles – simply because I showed them the respect they deserved. Overall the freshmen felt better, which made our school better.

There's a gift in all of us. We owe it to ourselves to keep searching. We should learn never to settle when it comes to being the best in this once-in-a-lifetime chance. During this time, my attitude was better, my outlook was better, and deep down inside I knew that good was going to come out of everything. I began to think, just like one of the World's Greatest Values, every day was an opportunity to become the best me I could be. As I became more successful, I took more pride in who I was and in everything I did. During my sophomore year, when I decided to strive to be my best, I made the varsity football team, the varsity basketball team, the wrestling team, varsity track, sophomore class president, and a peer mentor for other students. Teachers started to recognize me as an ambassador of my high school. The best "me" that I could be continued to get better as years followed. The next two years, I was junior class president and ASB president of the school. When someone asks me, "Why were you so successful during your high school career?" the first thing I say is, "My teachers." My teachers said it was the effort, willingness, and positive attitude I had that allowed them to help me. But if it wasn't for the inspiration I received from my teachers and the hope they gave me, I know I would not have had the high school career I did. More importantly, I am the best me because my teachers believed in me until I had the courage to believe in myself. Because of my high school career, my life just continued to get better. I no longer surrounded myself with troublemakers. I surrounded myself with people who helped me get better. Will you help others around you become better human beings?

In college at Chico State, I connected to all my

professors. One in particular, named Dr. Guzzly, helped me be the best me I could be. She believed we should never settle for anything and should always strive to be our best. I'll never forget the time I met her during office hours and I was extremely discouraged. I wanted to take a semester off of school, but she wouldn't have it. Dr. Guzzly told me that if I took a semester off, more than likely I would drop out of college. I explained to her that I was not as smart as the other students in class. She replied, "I know." I laughed and looked at her and said, "What do you mean?" Then she said, "Those students in class one day will end up with the job, but you're going to have a dream." I responded by saying, "I need a job." She laughed. Then she told me, "A job stands for 'just over broke.' You don't want to have a job; you want to have a dream. A dream is when you do something that you love to do, and you would do it for free, but you do it so well you get paid for it." This, to me, is a great example of being your best: not being something that society or someone else tells you to be but being authentically hard working and, in spite of your imperfections, striving to do your best.

I wanted to be an inspirational speaker, but I was scared. There were times when I did not believe in myself. I thought, "Who is going to ever hire a person to speak and make others feel good?" Every time I doubted myself, I thought of all those who believed in me: Dr. Guzzly, Dr. Avazino, Mr. Rizzi, Mr. Estrada, Miss Moles, Mr. Bright, and Ms. Clark. When I was a freshman, Ms. Clark gave us homework, and I was frustrated. So, in front of the class, I said, "This is stupid." She said something I will never forget. She said, "Keith, what you think is what you become." It's times like this that help make me the best person I can be. It's times like this that I think we all should use our dreams for strength when life challenges try to discourage us.

I have accomplished my high school dream by becoming one of America's top inspirational speakers. My accomplishments started when I chose to be the greatest me. Even in the harshest environment, where the culture was poor, I made a choice to be better. In all of us is this desire to want "better" for ourselves and to believe in ourselves. No matter how hard it gets, you just have to dig deep and then dig deeper! When you do this, your life will change for the better, and you will help make everyone around you better.

We all have a future. Every day is an opportunity to work on that future. We just need to remember that we are a gift to this world. You will never be duplicated. So, why not strive to be your greatest?

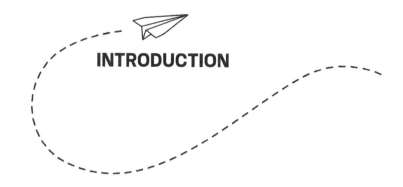

ROSE PETAL MOMENTS

"Create significant moments where everyone matters at your school."

We are so excited that you are holding this book in your hands.

Through the following pages of this short book, we know that you and the other students in your daily life will be greatly blessed. This book is not world-changing: You are. This book will show you how to change your life and the lives of those who surround you each day.

The thesis of this book is simple: By helping others around you become the best versions of themselves they possibly can be, you too can become your World's Greatest Me. By investing in the well-being of others, helping them become one step (or more) better than the day before, you are looking beyond your own self-interest into the well-being of the community that surrounds you; that's called "leadership."

Are you a leader? When working with high school and junior high school leadership students, I often ask this question in the classroom. Most of the time, there are a few people – just a few – who shoot their hands up as fast as possible. Simultaneously, most people simply look around the room to see the reaction of others. "Am I a leader?" they are asking themselves. From the standpoint of the book that you hold in your hands, you are a leader. If you are reading this book, you are a leader. Most people are reluctant to pick up the title of "leader" and tell others about it. There are many reasons for this, but there is one reason that usually stands above the rest. The reason that most people don't want to proclaim themselves as leaders is that it somehow feels "wrong."

"Do I have the right to draw all this attention to myself?" you might ask.

"Do I have the right to put myself in a position above others?" you may consider.

The purpose of a student leader is not to draw attention to oneself or to be in a position above others. Instead, the *purpose of a student leader is to serve others and create moments of significance where everyone matters at your school.* In short, you are a student leader if you want to (1) be of service and (2) make everyone clearly experience being needed and wanted at your school. Are those things that you want for others? Are those things you want for yourself?

Further, to be a student leader, you need to be a

leader of your "self" as well. This book will provide you with opportunities to become a better human being and to help others do the same. This will require you to experience discomfort, like the kind you experience when you physically exercise or do a tough homework assignment. Despite the momentary hardships that you may experience by challenging yourself and uplifting others, the payoffs will be lifelong for both you and the people you are seeking to ultimately assist.

Most of all, as a student leader, you need to be able to see the world through the eyes of others. We see our lives through the perspective of our experiences. This book will challenge you to start thinking about how other people are experiencing daily life at your school. Then, you'll be encouraged to make the changes necessary around you to assist others to see that they are needed and wanted at your school. Are you ready to see the world and those around you differently than you have before?

What Is It Like at Your School?

If your school is anything like many in the Western world, it's possible to go an entire day without feeling noticed and appreciated. School can feel more like a train station, with strangers rushing from one thing to another, than a place where people come together to become their best selves. Many years ago, one of my students told me that the entire previous year he did not think a single teacher knew his name – and he felt as if no one in his classes knew him either. When one stands in the hallways in between classes, one can see the type of emotion on people's faces. Some people are walking with others, talking. Others are walking through the hallways, making eye contact with friends and saying "hi." Many are simply keeping their heads down and rushing from one place to another. Quite similarly, if one walked the halls during lunchtime, one would see various collections of students eating together, with many others walking around while eating their food alone. School events, like rallies, can be quite difficult as well. Time and time again, the same groups of people are brought forward for praise, and many students know that they rarely, if ever, will be called forward to be part of the celebration. They are forced to sit and watch others matter.

As a student leader, it's your task to start noticing how people are being treated around you. Is every person being treated like a long-awaited guest to a party where they are loved and appreciated? Or, alternatively, are many people going through their day without anyone noticing them, appreciating them, and rewarding them for being part of the school family? It's also your task to create moments of significance where students feel like they matter.

Rose Petal Moments

A couple months ago, Park was visiting a high school in the Pacific Northwest, when he noticed a moment of significance unfolding. As he was walking up to the front door of the school, he noticed a skinny junior fellow standing with a container full of rose petals, a bouquet of flowers, a huge candy bar, and a giant stuffed panda bear. The young man looked excited and nervous as other male and female friends of his were gathering around him. An event was about to unfold! A significant moment! Other people were noticing too, as dozens and dozens of people started to stand and watch from the ground and the second-story balcony that overlooked the school's foyer area. Park wondered what was going on until he saw the six-foot-tall sign hanging from the balcony: "PROM?" the sign read. The young man started to create a walkway of rose petals. The entrance gave the appearance of a carpet of flowers. As he laid the last rose petal on the ground, he was ready to create this "Rose Petal Moment." The crowd suddenly got quiet as a few of the girls whispered loudly, "Here she comes!"

A young lady walked up to the entrance doors and stopped at the carpet of rose petals. You could see there was a moment of awareness on her part. She stopped just prior to the rose petal carpet and paused, looking quite puzzled by the crowd of people that was gathering. She then saw her boyfriend standing in the foyer with the bouquet of flowers, the candy bar, and the panda bear. She saw her group of students standing around this young man. She then realized that something significant was going to happen and that significant moment was for her. "This is about me?" she thought. When she looked up and saw the sign ("PROM?"), her look of confusion turned into a smile, laughter, and some tears. She walked over to her boyfriend, and he proudly asked her if she would go to the prom with him. "Yes," she nodded her head, "I'll go to prom with you," as she gave him a hug and a kiss. The crowd cheered and started to clap as everyone started to go on with their business for the day.

Imagine what it was like for her to walk into this scene. Already, when she walked into the foyer, it was clear that something out of the ordinary was happening. "What's all this?" she was probably thinking. When she noticed her friends were part of whatever was going on, she probably thought, "This has something to do with me!" However, when she finally saw her young man with the gifts and the sign, it was absolutely clear that she was not only part of this moment of significance: she was its chief recipient. This whole Rose Petal Moment was for her! Even the details were for her. The huge candy bar, the panda bear, and the roses were all items that were specifically picked out for her. They were of significance to her. Her friends being part of it made it even more meaningful because people she cared about were witnessing this moment with her. Without a doubt, she will remember this significant moment created specifically for her (her "Rose Petal Moment") for the rest of her life. She'll remember that more than what she learned in language arts that day! When she's an old lady, her grandson or daughter will ask her if she went to prom, and she'll remember this moment. For her, this will be one of the most important moments of her life. This Rose Petal Moment was specifically manufactured for her – for her benefit.

Conversely, imagine what it was like for someone who did not feel connected to this event at all. While everyone else was watching and celebrating, few people noticed the young man with the camouflage jacket and camouflage hat walking up. As he approached the front doors and the carpet of rose petals, he paused and noticed them. Watching his facial expression, you could see his reaction was, "Oh, this is going to be a significant moment, and it is not about me." It was clear that something out of the ordinary was happening. He then proceeded to walk around the rose petal carpet, making sure not to step on a single petal. He then walked over to the gathering of students that was now a few hundred people deep. As he approached the group of students, no one acknowledged him. No one said, "Good morning" or "What up!" In fact, no one moved aside as he tried to walk through the crowd.

For him, this was a significant moment as well. Nothing about this moment was for this "Camo Kid." This was probably just another day of feeling like he was not a significant member of the school. Imagine his memories of being at this school! "No one even said hello." No one acknowledged his presence. He knew he did not matter and that he would probably never experience a "Rose Petal Moment" like this at his school.   As a student leader, your entire duty can be summed up by saying this: create **Rose Petal Moments** – moments of significance crafted specifically for those you serve. Create significant moments where everyone matters at your school. Don't just say it. Live it!

Why This Book Matters

You have textbooks for math, English, science, history,

and a host of other subjects. Chances are, however, you've never had a leadership textbook in your hands. Leadership is not something that can be accomplished through an equation – though certain formulas can be helpful. Further, leadership is not like literature or history – though stories have much to do with the leaders we can and do become. Leadership is not a science alone – it's often a messy mix of both art and science. This book attempts to do what many others have failed to do: We are providing you (and your instructor) with the raw materials from which you can make the commitment to become a leader in your school and do what it takes to make significant moments for you and those around you. Take time to ask yourself, "What can I do today to make someone feel that they are significant? What can I do to help others 'Explore Their Greatness'?"

First, this book will allow you to consider what type of school you attend. You'll see how the daily life at your school is either helping or hindering students, teachers, parents, staff members, etc. to live a better life each day.

Second, this book will present to you the values of the World's Greatest High School, a school where each person is helping others to become their World's Greatest Me each day. You'll be provided with actual steps that you can take to make your life and the lives of those around you better.

Finally, this book will challenge you to fully embrace your status as a leader using your personal strengths.

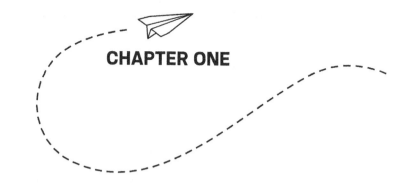

CHAPTER ONE

GRADUATION DAY EYES

"In whose life have I mattered? In what ways do I hope that I mattered?"

What if today was graduation day? What if today was the last day that you were required to be on a school campus for the rest of your life? Sure, you will probably go on to university – but what would it be like knowing that *today* was the last day that you would ever have to go to school without it being 100% your choice? Imagine what it would feel like to wake up knowing that today was the last. Imagine what it would be like to walk to class and interact with your peers and teachers. Imagine what lunch would taste like. Imagine what it would be like to be looking at the clock, knowing that in only a matter of minutes, the school year would be coming to a final close – a close that would never require you to return to campus again. Imagine that this was the last day: the culmination of all the hard work that you had done over the past thirteen or more years. All that work is about to pay off. What if today was your last day?

What would matter to you most today? Knowing that today is that last day that you would be spending on campus, what would deserve your attention most? Would you give your assignments their best? If you were in a physical education class, would you make the "warm-up" the best you had ever done? Would you run to the lunch line, or would you walk slowly? Would you be focused more on the tasks that were at hand, or would you be more focused on the people around you? Perhaps both? Consider that the people around you each day would probably look quite different on the last day. Knowing that this may, under most circumstances, be the last time that you would see most of these people, you might see them with greater patience and caring. If today was the last day of school, forever, what would matter most to you today?

Who would matter most to you today? Would you want to spend time connecting and talking with your friends? What would you want to make sure that you said to these individuals? What about your educators? Is there anything that you would want to make sure to say to them as well? If today was the last day at this school, to whom would you want to speak? To apologize? To ask for forgiveness? To confess your feelings? Imagine that this was the best opportunity for you to tell these human beings anything that you needed to say: What would you want to say to them? On the flip side, who do you hope would turn to you and have something to say? What do you hope people would say to you on such a day as this? Today, would you hope that someone would turn to you and say...

"I want to thank you for being a friend to me when..."

"I'm sorry about that one time that I..."

"You've meant more to me than I have told you before, because..."

"My life would not be the same without you, because..."

"Would you be willing to forgive me for that one time..."

"I'll never forget when..."

and many other such statements? In your mind right now, consider these questions: *In whose life have I mattered? In what ways do I hope that I mattered?* While so much of one's time as a student is spent considering the future and what one hopes he or she will enjoy in life after graduation, little time is dedicated to asking what one hopes he or she created with and for others around him or her. Most often, it's in the final moments of school that students stop thinking about what they accomplished and focus most upon with *whom* they accomplished – they begin to focus upon who mattered most to them. In these final moments, they think, "How did I matter?"

Have you looked at your school and the people in it with **graduation day eyes**? These are the eyes that you have when you sit in your chair at graduation, right next to the red carpet leading to the stage, and look in front of you and behind you, examining the faces of those whom you have seen for much time wandering the halls each school day. These are the eyes that know that these are the final moments of a chapter of life. These are the eyes that have experienced the entire story except the final page. As you sit at graduation and prepare to stand and walk onto the stage, you are reading the final page of "my school story." Imagine looking at every person with the knowledge that your part in their story is most likely ending today. You might see them in some other part of life later on, but this final chapter is about to close. Looking at your life with these eyes (even when you are a middle-schooler, freshman, or sophomore), you begin to experience what so many graduates have recounted: When you look at others with graduation day eyes, you realize how important you all are to each other. You all played some role in one another's lives. As you get called forward to a new class, a new grade, or even to the graduation stage, the more you put on these eyes, the more clearly you will see: You matter. We matter.

Imagine, at graduation, being called forward – you and your peers standing from your chairs, moving to one of the side aisles, and walking toward the stage in your caps and gowns. Your heart is pumping, so much so that you can barely hear what is happening around you. It's like you're floating to the stairs. When you take the first step onto the stage, as you reach for the railing, it is said that this is where you truly, for the first time, feel the full emotion of the moment. When you are there, you know this part of your story is coming to an end. The final moments, including the diplomas, are in sight. One by one, your peers in front of you are called onto the stage after they climb. As you are about to be called, you are feeling the emotion of your accomplishment. You think, "I did it."

Your name is called, and it's the moment you have been waiting for. You step onto the stage and begin walking through the final seconds of your high school career – you are about to get your diploma. You are graduating. It's at this moment that you look around you and see the hundreds, if not thousands, of individuals at the graduation ceremony. Faces and faces of individuals you know well, some you know a little bit, and many others you have never noticed before. You realize that you are part of the story of all the individuals around you. You realize that these students, these parents, and these educators, in some way, helped you get onto this stage. You realize that you also helped all these individuals, even if in the smallest of ways, make it here as well. You think, "We did it."

Diploma in hand, the first step down off the stage is the most important. This is the first step into the next era of your life. The new story is about to begin. Consider what it will be like to be about to take this final step, knowing that the door will be closed on your K-12 career forever. What regrets would you have if you walked off that stage today? Is there anything to which you need to attend before your final moment? Look at everyone and everything in your life today. What if today was graduation day? Would you be ready to leave most of these people and things behind? Or is further preparation required? The first step down from the stage is the most important, because it's the step that you can take saying, "I am leaving with no regrets."

What if today was graduation day? You don't have to wait until the last day to see things with such eyes. What will you do today? What will we do today? Will we leave with no regrets?

Who Are You? Who Are We?

As a student leader, train in having graduation day eyes. Look at your school life like a book where every page, every word matters. Look at your school life like a book that is about to end and deserves your full attention. It's your book, after all.

When we reach the end of a chapter of our lives, we do three things. First, we look back to those who have helped us here. Second, we look to who and what is important to us now. Finally, we look to whom and what we are walking toward. Whether you realize it or not, you are already in the final chapter of some area of your life. Consider what you and those around you were like just two years ago. What about four years ago? Six? Likewise, consider what life will be like in the coming months and years. You are in a closing season of life. Soon, you will be in a new season, heading swiftly toward another close. These short chapters provide you with a brief window in which you can do that which will benefit you and others most. After the chapter is gone, the opportunities are gone, or at least greatly changed. You can be an ambitious freshman in the ninth grade, but it's hard to be a hard-working freshman when you are in the twelfth grade. Likewise, it's possible to help other middle-schoolers or high-schoolers around you when you are in middle school or high school. However, it's quite different to help these same people when you are in college or beyond. They say (whoever "they" are), "You are only young once." Another way to say this is, "You are only *you* now, *now.*" This chapter of life is about to end, and you will never be the same. What will you do before it does? Who will you help while you can?

Who has helped you get to this point in your life? Who has supported you? Think about all the peers who have helped you become who you are and do what you have done. Think about the educators who have had a part in your unfolding story. Think about those who have taken care of you where you call home and beyond. What have you done to recognize and thank these people while you are in this chapter of your life? What has been left unsaid that needs to be said? If you graduated today and this chapter closed, what regrets would you have? Quite similarly, what have you done to support your own desires for your life during this chapter? What has been accomplished? What did you do? Conversely, what has not yet been done? What do you need to do before it's too late? Look back and recognize what and who has allowed you to sit where you are sitting at this moment. Your past has made you who you are today.

What about today? What is important to you today? Who is important to you today? Think about the present moment in this chapter of your life. The activities and persons in your life whom you consider most important deserve your attention as well. Think about the goals toward which you are working each day and the people who are working alongside you in similar goals. What are you doing each day toward these goals? How are you making your goals more and more likely to come to fruition each day? What *today* has not yet been done that needs your immediate attention? Likewise, who needs your assistance today? Who cannot fulfill their goals without your involvement? As you consider these things, know that, as you are reading this, time still remains to make this the best day ever. As you look to today, look with graduation day eyes: Who you are today and how you are with others today can make you more like the man or woman you want to be.

What about the future? Whom and what are you walking toward? Think about the kind of people you want to meet in your future. Think about the type of people you want to work with each day. Similarly, consider what you want to have, be, and do in the future. Each day is the opportunity to take one step (or more) toward these people and goals. At school, much of your time has been dedicated to the question, "Where are you headed?" Consider, however, that rather than looking at where you are headed in five years, ten years, or beyond, there is much value in simply looking to where you are headed in the next chapter of your life (even if that chapter is only six months away). As you read this, you may be closing the chapter of your freshman and sophomore years. You may be closing the chapter called "middle school." You could be closing the school life chapter altogether and are getting ready to graduate and go to university. Regardless, know that everything you do can contribute to the next chapter of your life. Likewise, each thing you do can have a negative impact upon it.

You are about to end this chapter of your life. Today, you could recognize those (including yourself) who have allowed you to be here. Today, you could see where you are and use this day to make yourself and others around you better human beings. Today, you could look ahead to the next chapter of life and make sure that you are going to be moving on with no regrets.

Consider that in just a short number of months or years, you too will be sitting amongst so many of your peers and educators in a cap and a gown. You will look around you and recognize that each person around you has played some role in your school life (and you have played a role in all their school lives as well). Will you be able to say, "I did it"?

You will stand and step onto the grad stage and see all the people celebrating with you and all those who helped one another to get there. Will you be able to say, "We did it"?

You will be taking your first step off that stage. Will you be able to say, "I leave with no regrets"?

The choice is yours – but those around you can help you choose and help you find the way. Likewise, you can help those around you as well. You can help all your fellow students make the choice to become better today than yesterday and take one more bold step toward their graduation day.

Meet Chris

Like you, Chris was nearing the end of such a chapter in

his life. He had just completed his junior year of high school and was enjoying his summer before starting the final ten-or-so months of class before graduating. He was having the time of his life, spending time with his family at the lake, doing martial arts, and starting the early preparations for his college applications. Already finished were twelve years of his grades K-12 school life. When September hit, he would only have ten more months left of class. After that, he would move on to college. Anything was possible. One day, as he was going down the road in his white truck, he was not paying attention to what was behind him in the rear-view mirror. However, down that road he had just traveled was a family that loved him, a group of friends who were thankful for his friendship, and lots of educators (at his school) who were helping him every day become the man he wanted to be. Life was great. Soon, this chapter of life would be ending. Soon, he would graduate.

What chapter of your life is soon to be ending? You could be reading this and be a middle-schooler, about to move on to the adventures of high school and beyond. You could be a freshman or sophomore student ready to move on to the higher grades so you can finish and move on. You could be a high school junior, just one year away from becoming a senior, applying to university or considering other options for post-high-school life. Likewise, you could be a high school senior in the throes of sending applications to prospective schools, finishing your final year, and getting ready for the biggest change of life that you have ever experienced: graduation. Think about all that has happened in your life to date that has allowed or encouraged you to become the person you are today. In many ways, perhaps you are quite fortunate to have had the life experience that would allow you to sit in such a place as you are sitting right now, reading this book. You could be anywhere on the planet – but here you are. Soon, this chapter will end and you will be moving onto the next chapter. Like Chris, you could look into that rear-view mirror and see all that's behind you. What is in the mirror of the past? What has happened to allow you to sit here today?

Likewise, who has contributed to make you into the person you are today? Who are the people who have supported you up to this point in your school life? Who has made it possible for you to sit here today? Consider, for a moment, the gratitude that you feel toward these individuals. You could be in places far different from this if it were not for these people. What are the names and faces that come to mind as you consider these questions? So many people help make a person. When you look back, there are dozens upon dozens of educators who went to work each day simply to make it possible for you to be "you" today. Likewise, there may be people in your life whom you consider "family" who did whatever they could, in small and big ways, to make sure that you were able to sit in this chair, desk, or couch today. Who has helped you become the man or woman that you are? Like Chris, who is behind you supporting you?

At fifty miles per hour, he was cruising his truck down the main drive of his city, when red and blue flashing lights brought him out of his happy state into one of concern and surprise. It was a police officer in a cruiser who was clearly expecting Chris to pull over to the side. In one instant, Chris was taken from the excitement of the day and all that had led to it into the reality that he had, potentially, broken the law in some way. Walking up to the side of Chris's truck, the police officer looked at Chris through the car's mirror. After rolling down his window and speaking to the office, Chris realized that he was probably speeding. The police officer was quite curious about where Chris was going in such a hurry – especially when he saw that Chris was wearing a uniform.

"I'm headed to the lake to join my friends," Chris said nervously to the police officer. At the lake, Chris was joining hundreds of his friends who were part of an adventure organization. The gathering was a huge outdoor party with competitions, food, and friendship. The officer squinted his eyes under his glasses before speaking.

"Watch how fast you are going down this hill next time," said the officer in a strong tone, "and have fun." He turned and returned to his police cruiser and drove away. As Chris started his engine and continued his journey to the highway, he was again filled with a sense of thanks. Life had some unplanned interruptions, but it was good. He was on the road to his destination.

What do you have today to be thankful for? Think about what in your life is helping you more and more become the person whom you are wanting to become. Think about those things in your life that are helping you do the things that you want more and more each day.

Think about what you want to have in life and about how your work and the work of so many others around you is helping you get those things. Though there may be some unexpected interruptions in your day, these things that you are thankful for are still there.

What challenges are you facing today? Consider what is preventing you from having, being, and doing what you want today. Consider all the factors in your life that are not helping you work toward being the best version of yourself possible. Consider those people and situations that seem to reduce your ability to make your life all that you want it to be. Are these situations permanent? Temporary?

Just as Chris was headed on a journey this certain day to a huge gathering of friends, before going onto his final year of high school, to graduation, and beyond, you too are on a road toward your next destination. As the chapter of this life begins to close, consider where you are headed. Where are you headed? What challenges are you going to soon face for which you must prepare?

Today Matters at the World's Greatest High School

Few guarantees are provided to us in life. Chances are, for years, you have been listing your goals for the future to yourself, fellow students, and adults alike. You have probably had dozens, if not hundreds, of conversations about "what I want to be when I grow up." Already, it's highly likely that your plans have changed a few times. Interests fade. New pursuits become one's focus. However, even though much of our desires tend to change, there are probably a few hopes and dreams that have not changed much at all. Each person, especially as he or she starts moving through high school, tends to see that he or she has specific gifts, talents, and skills. Students like you and Chris often build your hopes and dreams upon these abilities and capacities. At the same time, are you guaranteed to get into the college of your fantasies or land that dream job? No. However, there is much you can do to help you get there.

Without a doubt, we have today – we have this moment. The **World's Greatest High School** is a place where every person within it is becoming his or her personal best each day. We call this "personal best" one's **World's Greatest Me**. Imagine coming to a school where the hope and dream of every person and the actual work that was done each day was only to help yourself and others advance in becoming your World's Greatest Me. Though there may be no guarantees that you will get into that university that you are dreaming about, in such a school – in fact, in your school – you could work today to be one step better than yesterday. If, each day, you reach to be one moment, one step, one conversation, one action better than the day before, you are slowly but surely becoming the best version of yourself: your World's Greatest Me. Can you say, "I gave my personal best today"?

We can decide who we want to be today. It's much harder to decide who we want to be three years or ten years from now. Who knows what will be happening around us in a few days, much less years down the line? Planning for the future is great; however, even better, and the subject of this book, is helping yourself and others take one step toward being your World's Greatest Me each day. Think about the other people who are in the same room in which you are sitting right now or in the same building as you are. All of these people are going somewhere in life; no one goes "nowhere." Some people will be going on to be amazing parents. Some will go on to help others at a business, school, or elsewhere. Others will go on to be creators, writers, artists, athletes, leaders, etc. A few may be going toward disaster, jail, or worse. Regardless, everyone is going somewhere. You are going somewhere. While there's no guarantee that you will get where you expect, what you can guarantee is how you are in the world at this very moment. With yourself, you could be your World's Greatest Me and finish your reading assignment. With others, you could make eye contact and ask them how they are doing. Basically, one thing that is guaranteed is that you *could* be your World's Greatest Me right now in this moment, today. So, what do you need to be or do right now to be one step better than before? That's what leaders do: they help themselves and others be their personal best right now.

So, what do you want to be today? What do you want to be right now? Perhaps you want and need to be the type of person who is going to finish this paragraph or section of this book. Alternatively, maybe you have other things to which you need to attend (we're excited that you would take some time out of your schedule to read this). A friend may be sitting nearby and needs a shoulder to cry on – and you just so happen to be the type of person who wants to comfort others or, at least, comfort this friend. You may want to be an athlete and know that you need to get on that track, field, pool, etc. or need to get in that gym. You may want to be an artist and have an instrument or tool that needs to be picked up. With all that's clamoring for your attention as a human being, what deserves the most attention right now that would allow you to be your World's Greatest Me?

What we do contributes to being our World's Greatest Me. So much emphasis in school is placed on goals. Goals are ideas about where we want to go, typically in the long-term days, weeks, months, or years ahead. If you're like most people, goals get changed when other, better ideas become your goals or when you miss meeting your goals entirely. So, what's a goal worth if we don't accomplish it? When you are working each day to become your World's Greatest Me, what you are doing *right now*, today, becomes of the greatest concern. For example, if you want to be the best friend you can be to someone who's in pain today, that person doesn't need you tomorrow – he or she needs you today! If you need to be the best student you can be in your English class today, there's no sense in putting off doing the work that you need to do until tomorrow – it's today that matters most. So, stop reading this for a second and ask yourself, "What do I need to do right now to be my World's Greatest Me?" You may decide that reading on in this book is what you need. You may decide that, instead, something else requires your immediate attention. Imagine what it would be like to go through the rest of the day simply asking this question of yourself each moment. When you are walking in between classes, imagine wanting to be your personal best, walking between classes making eye contact with other people, talking and listening with a friend. Perhaps during lunch you want to be your personal best while eating your lunch, so you eat slowly and actually taste your food. Perhaps right now you want to be the best reader you can be, so you slow down and actually read each of these sentences. This logic goes on and on. What you do *right now* is helping you become your World's Greatest Me. You don't have to wait until tomorrow or the start of the new year to make a resolution. Your journey to become the best self you can be starts right now. Just as Chris was loving life, on the road to do that which he wanted to do most that day, you can *right now* be on the road to being what you want to be most. The steps you take now are far more important than the destination five or ten years from now.

We can't get there alone, however. We can't become the best versions of ourselves without being assisted by others. Likewise, you can't be your World's Greatest Me without helping others. Becoming your personal best is a team sport. The reason the school that you attend works is that people come together to help one another. Now, imagine if your school as a whole decided to help each person inside of it become their World's Greatest Me. Like we mentioned above, we call such a place the World's Greatest High School. We'll talk about this type of school later in this volume. For now, simply know that other people have to be part of your journey of becoming your World's Greatest Me. After all, a hero cannot be a hero without a village to call home and save. A hero cannot be a hero unless someone wiser instructs him or her. A hero cannot be a hero without a dragon to slay. Others are always part of the equation of becoming your personal best. You could not be here today without other human beings. You could not go anywhere without others either. Quite similarly, people need you. They need you to be the best version of yourself so that you can help them become the same. Others need your help. You need the help of others.

"We" Matter

Together, a group can do far more than one can do alone. How far in your education could you get without the textbooks that you use each day that were created by hundreds of individuals? How far in your day could you get without the thousands of individuals who contributed to your mode of transportation, the road, or the signs on it? How much could you eat today without the even greater number of individuals who were part of planting, feeding, growing, and preparing the food? Simply put, without others, you could not be your World's Greatest Me, unless you wanted to be your World's Greatest Me in a hand-built cabin somewhere with no electricity, created with tools that you forged yourself from rocks. You need others to grow. You need others to pursue your dreams. So, the other students who are around you each day aren't simply other human beings trying to get diplomas: They are people who can help you, and they need your help. Just as much as you matter, "we matter." As student leaders, you, together, can make the decision to help others become their World's Greatest Me while becoming the same.

Who do you want to be together with your peers? Do you want to be a leadership team that is celebrating the same celebrities of your campus each week or month? Or do you want to be the leadership team that recognizes the unrecognized, daily heroic actions of students who are working to become their World's Greatest Me? Do you want to be a leadership team that is made up of a group of people largely here only to serve their self-interests and get a qualification to put on their college applications? Or do you want to be the leadership team that is in the life business of serving others for the sake of being of service? Do you want to be the leadership team that comes together to throw dances, paint posters, and hand out awards every now and then? Or do you want to be the type of leadership team that is becoming better and better each day at helping each person on campus explore his or her greatness? Do you want to be a leadership team that carries a badge of superiority and power above other students? Or do you want to be the leadership team whose purpose is to empower others, potentially at a cost?

Why is it that we often wait for hardship to wake us up and truly recognize what's important to us? Perhaps you have experienced a disaster or a difficult time in your own life. Perhaps you have witnessed someone else experiencing a difficult (if not the most difficult) moment in his or her life. When someone close to us dies, gets dearly injured, or succumbs to an addiction or sickness, it's often at this time that our priorities become clear. During these times, we often say things like...

"I wish I made the time to spend more time with that person,"

"I should have been more kind to them,"

"I could have given them my undivided attention," or

"I truly missed out – now it's too late."

We don't need to have a horrible thing happen to us or those we love for us to see what truly matters. Each person who is sitting around you, if you think about it, matters quite dearly to you. They may not be your best friend. They may not be family. Maybe they are! Regardless, by simply thinking about what "really matters," you can see that the people who are part of your life each day matter. They matter because you are helping them become their best. They matter because they are helping you become your personal best. Now, think about the people outside your classroom or home who are part of your daily life – even if they are simply passing you in the hallway or the street. Do these people not matter in some way as well? Even simply by being part of your school community, are they not also important? When you begin to think in this way and start seeing the connection we have with one another, you begin to realize that each person around you matters. More to the point, together, "we matter."

To what degree are you willing to wake up and work hard today on behalf of yourself and others around you? You and the people around you don't need you to be your worst today; you and others need you to be just a little better than you were yesterday. In fact, others will do more poorly around you if you are not playing your game as your personal best. They will do more poorly when you are not being the better student you can be, not coexisting as a better citizen of your school, or not being the better friend that you could potentially be. Without a doubt, you have had situations in a classroom where other students have distracted you from your ability and right to learn. When another student goofs off, purposely makes the teacher angry, or all-out does something inappropriate, this has an easily seen impact upon you. When that student was not being his or her personal best, you were worse for it. If you take this exact logic and apply it to you being a student leader, you can begin to see that you being your World's Greatest Me, just one step better than yesterday, is what others around you need most. They need you so much that they can't even see it. Will you show them your better self?

One can decide to make a change in life, or one can be changed by life. If you've witnessed others going through hardship, you know that some people are able to carry on and survive, whereas others crumble, never to recover. You may even know of someone who thrived in the hardship! What allows one person to continue on, even when it's hard, and still continue to get better and better each day after life takes an (often) unexpected turn? Quite similarly, everyone who sits in your language arts class, your math class, or your science class gets the same teacher, but some are able to do fine, some are able to do well, and others crumble. What makes one student able to do well while another has significant difficulty and another drops out of school? There are many answers to these questions. However, here are some things that we often observe:

1. Those becoming their World's Greatest Me are, themselves, working each day to explore their greatness and be one step better than yesterday; and

2. Those becoming their World's Greatest Me have others, even in the smallest of ways, helping them explore that greatness and become better human beings.

So, you can choose to make one thing, anything, better than yesterday. You also can choose to assist others in their journey. This is student leadership. This is your "personal best." Even when hardship hits, you can meet challenges as your personal best. Could you imagine living life where even the hard stuff becomes the foundation from which your personal best could emerge? What if difficulty could be the training ground for the best you ever?

Finishing the Chapter

Our friend Chris arrived to the lake, ready to join hundreds of others in his adventure organization in games and competition. By the middle of the day, it was time for Chris to compete with his team in the relay race. He changed out of his uniform into swim trunks and headed out to the lake with his friends who were on his team. As he stepped up to the challenge that he was about to face, he felt the hot sun and wind on his skin, walking down to the edge of the lake. The crowds of hundreds of other fellow teenagers advanced to the edge of the lake to see this part of the relay race begin. Chris, a strong swimmer, would be waiting for his partner to run up from the water and hand him a baton before he ran into the water himself. As the racers began taking their marks, Chris felt the adrenaline begin to build within his body. His pulse began to advance as he was getting ready.

"GO!" shouted the referee. Chris watched the first round of guys run down the sand, jump into the lake, and swim out to the buoy a few hundred feet off shore. As they circled the orange floating structure in the water, Chris's pulse began to raise, and his legs became restless. Soon, he would be handed the baton, and he would have to fly down the sand into the water and to the same buoy. He would swim as fast as he could, advancing as much as possible beyond the others. He would run up the shore and hand the object to his partner for the final round.

As the first swimmers began to return to shore, Chris realized that his partner and the member of another team were nearly tied. Chris felt even more energy in his body as he realized that he would have to give the best swim of his life to help his team win. His partner got to shore and started bolting toward Chris. Chris started moving his feet in place, almost trying to get a running start standing still. Finally, his partner reached out his hand with the baton and placed it into Chris's hand.

Chris was off as fast as he could go down the shore.

He began to breathe as deeply as he could to keep his pulse low and send much-needed oxygen to his muscles. His feet were hitting the sand perfectly, the padding of his feet to his toes, driving his body forward as fast as possible. The air was rushing past his ears such that he heard wind all over. Ahead, the water was inviting. Tensing his arms, he prepared to throw them out in front of him such that he could dive forward and get the best start to the water. He took two final steps as his ankles, calves, knees, and, finally, lower thighs hit the water. He leapt forward with his arms outstretched, his hands, elbows, and arms propelling him forward into the water.

He felt suddenly motionless.

He realized he was no longer moving in the water.

He was not entirely comprehending the feeling of cool aching in his head and neck.

He could not move. He could not breathe. He was under water.

Above him, he could hear the muffled cheering change. It sounded different. Lower. Primal. Urgent.

He could hear the murky, obscured voices of men yelling and drawing near.

He saw the dark water below him, as hands grabbed him and pulled him to the surface of the water and turned him over.

Chris did not understand.

Chris did not know until he woke up three weeks later that he had broken his neck.

BLUEPRINT QUESTIONS:

----

1. If today was the last day of school before graduation, what would you hope you had accomplished by today? What would you hope your student leadership team accomplished? Would you be leaving with regrets? If so, what would they be?

2. Who has helped you get to this point in your life? What is important to you today? Who is important to you today? Where are you headed?

3. Explain some ways in which you could be your World's Greatest Me today. What are some ways in which you could be one step better than yesterday?

4. Who needs you to be your best today *for them*? Who do you need to be his or her best today *for you*?

5. What is a student leader? What is the purpose of your student leadership team?

6. If you lived one hour today attempting to be your personal best, how would you feel if you accomplished your goal? What would you feel when you fell short? Why?

DARES:

----

1. Identify one other person in your class or school

whom you don't know well. Be one step better than yesterday with this person (say "hello," talk with him or her, hold the door for him or her, etc.). (Bonus: do this for someone you consider challenging.)

2. Identify one person in your life who has helped you become the person you are today. Write down what that person has done to help you. Go to this person and tell him or her "thank you" and how he or she has helped you become a better person. Before you go, ask yourself, "How did he or she make me feel significant in the past?"

3. Identify one thing in your life you want to do better today than yesterday. Do it.

4. Think about something you need from a friend, peer, teacher, someone at home, or anyone else who would help you do anything better than yesterday. Go to that person and ask for the help you need.

5. Write a letter of promise to yourself. What are the ways in which you will serve *you* this semester? What are some ways in which you will serve others this semester? Seal this letter in an envelope and write your name and home address on it. Hand it to your leadership teacher for safekeeping, asking him or her to mail it in a few months.

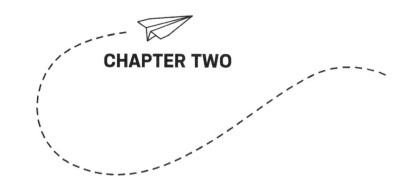

CHAPTER TWO

THREE TYPES OF SCHOOLS

"The purpose of school is to provide the conditions for growth and life as if 'all kids have futures.'"

Three weeks later, Chris began to wake up in the hospital. For three weeks, doctors purposely placed Chris in an induced coma so that he could receive the medical care he needed. As he began to slowly, over the course of many days, wake up, he did not know that his neck was broken. He did not know that his head struck an underwater sandbar that none of the race attendees or organizers knew was there. He did not know that he had broken his neck at his C4 vertebra a catastrophic injury that would most likely leave him fully paralyzed for the rest of his life. He did not know that he had been pulled from the water and taken by helicopter to the hospital. He did not know that he had been asleep for nearly a month's time. What he did know was that he couldn't move and that he was in a great deal of pain. As he began to wake up further, he knew that he was attached to tubes and machines: life support. He knew that he was dependent upon the help of others – without them, he could not survive. To what kind of world was Chris waking up?

Like Chris, so many students are thrust from the cradles of elementary school into middle school, from middle school into high school, or, possibly, from any school into a new one. When one arrives into such a new place, what does one experience? When one shifts swiftly into a new school, year, semester, or classroom, what does such a student experience? Naturally, there is a period of confusion. Surroundings are unfamiliar. People are unfamiliar. During this time, it's quite natural to ask, "Is this a friendly place? Are these people whom I can trust?" As a student (or anyone for that matter) comes into a new chapter of his or her school life, that student begins to realize what he or she is feeling in this place on an hourly and daily basis. The student might say to him- or herself, "I feel like I have to be very careful here not to say anything wrong!" Alternatively, he or she could say, "I feel like I'm not particularly welcome in this place." Accordingly, the feeling of being in this new place can be quite horrible. Worse yet, some students come into such a new school, year, semester, or classroom in a dangerous condition: academically, emotionally, or socially, they may be on life support. What kind of world will a new student find at your school this year? What kind of world will a new student find at your school this semester? What about inside your classroom? What kind of world will a new student find there? Will that new student find the type of world that can help him or her be well?

Your school is a powerful place. Many students will spend more waking hours on your campus than they will at home. What type of place is your school? How do you know it's that type of place? As Chris woke up, he was looking for clues as to what type of world he was waking up to. He was wondering, "Are these people around me going to help me? Am I safe? Is this the type of place and are these the type of people who can help me be well?" As students enter your school, they are asking themselves the same questions. Is your school the type of place where every student can say, "Yes, this is a place where I am safe, wanted, and appreciated"?

In this chapter, we will discuss how you can see your school such that you can decide what changes and enhancements are required. In the next chapter, we'll talk about how you personally can help these transformations.

School

What is a school? If you take a few minutes out of your day today and ask every single one of your teachers to define the word "school," you'll be sure (on most campuses) to find an interesting phenomenon: every teacher will have a different definition. Isn't that peculiar? There are probably somewhere between a dozen and a few hundred educators on your campus, and only a small few of them are utilizing the same operating definition of *school* – and yet they all work at one. Likewise, if you asked a few students during lunchtime this week for their definitions, you'd see that, while there would be some similarities in what they said, there is quite rarely an agreed-upon understanding of this word. Is it not best that a team (no matter what game they are attempting to play) be playing the same game? Is it not best that a team play by the same rules? Shouldn't they be playing for the same goals? Listening to the definitions of the educators and students on your campus, you'll see that many are playing entirely different games that they call *school*.

For the purposes of this book and, we suggest, for the purposes of your student leadership, we define **school** as **a place where people gather for the exploration and process of learning about the self and the universe**. School is the place where you go to learn about the world around you and to learn about yourself. Often, content classes like math, science, and language arts are the places where you learn about the world, how it functions, and how you and others function within it. Where, then, does one go specifically to explore oneself? If you are so fortunate to sit in a student leadership classroom under the direction of a qualified leadership teacher, then you are in the perfect place to begin learning about yourself. For most students, however, where do they learn about themselves in such a concentrated, purposeful place? Shouldn't school offer each student the chance to learn much about him- or herself inside and outside the classroom? Shouldn't this be one of the primary reasons that students come to school each day?

What is the purpose of a school? What is the purpose of your school? As with the definition of "school," you could go to many different individuals inside and outside your school and observe the myriad definitions offered. There is little consensus regarding why students go to school, for what purpose teachers are there, and, quite important to us, the purpose of student leadership on your campus. When you visit great schools throughout the country (and the world), you notice many common characteristics. One of the most pronounced attributes of such schools is the unified, agreed-upon purpose that these schools have adopted. Most of the individuals within the schools agree that school, while it has many purposes, has one overarching purpose that deserves a place above all others: **The purpose of school is to provide the conditions for growth and life as if "all kids have futures."** Schools allow students to explore. However, that exploration is not an unguided process where a few are successful and many others stay lost. Instead, great schools have intentionally modified their beliefs, actions, culture, and systems to ensure that students are most able to engage in such an exploration and become better human beings.

The Four C's

The philosopher Ken Wilber described human experience in terms of four distinct dimensions: what's inside me, outside me, inside us, and outside us. Likewise, it could be said that your experience of school is an interrelationship between these four distinct factors. When you look at a school, there is much going on. Even in a horrible school, each day there is a whole host of decisions, actions, tenets, and routines that form it. When you speak to people in your community, including educators, students, parents, and others, what is the reputation of your school? What words do they use to describe your school? Regardless of what is said by the posters on the wall, the banner at the front of the school, or the principal at the occasional rally or assembly, it's what *most* people say about your school that is probably closer to your school's true identity. Plenty of schools would prefer to spend a few hundred dollars to paint the words "best school" on the side of their building rather than doing the real work required to make their school truly "best" each day. What makes a school's identity is not what one person says it is – until the decisions, actions, tenets, and routines match that to the point where most people agree with the words of that one person. It's not about words; it's about what your school and the people within it prove day in and day out. For the purposes of the audience of this book, we have changed the names of Wilber's dimensions to be most useful in the high school student leadership team environment. Once you understand these four dimensions, you'll be able to truly see how your school is doing. We offer these dimensions as a way by which you, and your fellow leaders, can start the hard work that is ahead.

First, **cause** is defined as **those beliefs and values inside of a single person**. Think of this term like "I feel I am part of a *cause*" or "I believe in this *cause*." Cause includes any belief or value that you hold inside yourself: where values and beliefs are kept. If you believe that "every student is going somewhere," then that is part of your cause. If you think that "hard work will make me successful," that too is part of your cause. If you value "my team needs me to work hard," then this is also part of your cause. Your causes are all the beliefs and values inside of you. They form a special blueprint within your heart and mind that is quite unique. All your memories and experiences are inside of you and are part of what helps form this cause. Part of what makes you "you" is this collection of beliefs and values, influenced greatly by your past experience. Often, these are the source of what we do out in the world on a daily basis. However, remember: your cause is *inside* of you.

Before Chris found himself in the hospital, there already existed many parts of his cause that, in part, made him the soon-to-be high school senior that he was. He believed that "family is greatly important," and he loved his family very much. He valued "hard work and training," growing through athletics, and enjoying that which made him a better human being. He valued "being part of a team." He believed in himself. He believed in his family. He believed in his teammates. At the foundation of his heart and mind were these beliefs and values that, in part, made him the unique human being that he was. What about you? What do you believe? That is, what are those things that you know to be true about yourself, others, and life? What do you value? That is, what are those principles or ideals that you see as particularly important regarding yourself, others, and life? Inside of you, these create an inner world that is quite unique. Consider how this inner world has a profound impact on what you do in the world outside of yourself, in your classroom, in the hallways, and beyond.

The second C is "command." **Command** is defined as **the observable actions you take as an individual in the world**. While your cause exists inside of you where no one can see it, your *command* is those things that you actually do for yourself and others to see in the physical world. You could say that part of your command is "I did three homework assignments yesterday." Likewise, you could say that part of your command is "I got to school at 7:15 a.m. today." Similarly, you could say that "I am reading some text right now." All of these are examples of your command. Every day, you command hundreds of thousands (perhaps more) of actions. Some of these you do intentionally; some of them you don't even know that you are doing. The words you say out loud and the actions that you take are all part of your command because they happen in the physical world, and other people could potentially observe these actions.

Chris, at one point, attended martial arts classes. He sat with his eyes closed and meditated inside these classes. He swam. He threw a ball through a net. He attended class. All of these were part of his command of this life. There is an old adage, "Actions speak louder than words." Well, both actions and words are part of your command. However, this wisdom definitely seems to be verified by our observations of people around us. When someone says one thing but does another, we see that there is a mismatch. Accordingly, when someone believes or values one thing but does something in the world contrary to that belief or value, we could say that something appears to be in error. Think about the actions today that allowed you to be in this room. You woke up. You groomed yourself. You transported yourself to this place. You sat in this chair. All of these are part of your command. You did these things. What you do matters.

The third C is "conversation." **Conversation** is defined as **the observable actions you take with others at your school**. While command is about your action alone, *conversation* is about the actions that you and others take together in the physical world. When the bell rings at your school and all students start walking somewhere, that is a conversation of sorts. When you and another classmate turn to one another and start speaking, that is a conversation too. When you and your classmates turn in an assignment to a teacher together, that is a conversation. Likewise, when you and your fellow student leaders throw a celebration, run a rally, or undertake a ritual ceremony, these are all conversations. When two people physically argue or fight, this is a conversation (though not necessarily a very nice one). Every action you take with another human being or group of human beings is part of a conversation – even when it is a silent one, even when that conversation may seem like it's one of conflict. If you stepped into an elevator and buried your head in one of the corners, others who rode that elevator with you would think this quite odd, but it's a conversation nonetheless, because it's an action taken with other human beings.

Chris was part of a team of athletes engaged in a competition with others. That teamwork was a conversation. That competition was a conversation. The rules of the game and the following and breaking of those rules were a conversation. Think, for a moment, about the various conversations that happen at your school. Think about the speed at which most people walk to class. Think about the way that the lunch line looks. Think about the way that people speak to one another (if at all) in the hallways. Think about the way people act together at rallies, celebrations, etc. Think about the way that your team of student leaders functions or malfunctions. These are all part of a conversation: it's how people are acting in the world together.

Finally, the last C is "culture." **Culture** is defined as **those beliefs and values inside of many people at your school.** When many students at your school don't care about getting to school on time, that's part of your school culture. When many teachers value having as many students graduate as possible, that's culture too. When many parents believe that their students should have a safer school, that's part of your culture as well. Culture is any belief that many people have at your school, no matter how small that group of people. You could have a very small part of your culture that believes one thing, while a very loud majority of your culture can feel another: it's all part of the same culture. Another way of putting *culture* is "What do we believe together?" If you were to pose that question to your fellow student leaders around you, what sorts of answers would the group agree upon? Those answers are part of your culture as a team of student leaders. If you were to ask teachers together in the same room, "Do you think all students have a future?" the answers that you get are part of the culture of your school too.

Chris was part of a family that valued "being there" for one another through the good and the bad: this was part of the culture of his family. His family valued spending as much time together as possible. His family believed in Chris. His family loved each other. All of these things are part of the culture of Chris's family. When you look around your school, what do you think this school believes together? It may not be hard to imagine, because you may hear a lot of complaints about your school. On the other side, you may hear a great deal of praise about a specific teacher. Students may believe, in large, that your school is a great school – or a poor school. Regardless, those beliefs that people have *together* are known as culture.

Together (cause, command, conversation, and culture), we call these **the Four C's**. Consider these as a way to see more deeply into your school and the people within it. You can ask yourself, "What do I believe?" You could ask yourself, "What am I doing?" You could consider, "What am I doing with others?" You can ask yourself, "What do we believe?" Each of the answers to these questions has a profound impact upon how you experience your life. What happens if you apply the Four C's to examining your school?

The Three States

Take a moment and go through each of the Four C's. Ask yourself,

What do I believe about school?

What actions did I take today?

What actions did I take with others?

What do I and the people around me believe together?

When you start to look at the answers to these questions next to one another, you can perhaps get a distinct feeling or see some clear evidence of how you and your school are performing as a whole. It can be so easy for a student leader to make the mistake of saying, "My school is a good/bad school." That's too simplistic for a leader who wants to help him- or herself, his or her school, and the people in it become better and better. To serve your school, you have to be able to understand how to see the answers that you hear.

When you look into the Four C's of your school, you could see three possible states: No Hope, Mediocre, or World's Greatest. Collectively, we call these **the Three States**.

No Hope is defined as **change not possible and not wanted**. For example, a student who believes that he or she can never graduate and is unwilling to ever change is in a state of *no hope*. Similarly, if teachers at your school will not make the changes necessary to help more students pass and graduate, this too is a state of *no hope*. No hope will never result in change, because the conditions for change are not possible; things can't change, most often, because people don't want a change. This would be like a person believing and saying that he or she has no interest in being healthier, having the help of others to keep him or her unhealthy. While in a state of no hope, there is no possibility of change for such a person. This state is often characterized by people saying, "It's not possible for anything to get better here," and at the same time, "We don't want to change."

Think about someone in your life: Do you know a person who does not want to change and acts like change is not possible? Do you know others who truly should change, deserve to change, and it seems that change is not possible or welcomed? Think about your school. Are there things that need to improve but the improvements don't seem possible or wanted? If changes are not possible and are not wanted, then this is a state of no hope. Truly, it's one of the lowest, most depressing states that a person or persons can experience.

Mediocre is defined as *change possible but not wanted.* For example, a certain group of leaders may be acknowledging only a small handful of students at their school. They could bless more students, but they don't want to. They'd rather keep doing the "okay" job of acknowledging a few rather than doing the hard work to bless more. A mediocre attitude, indeed! Similarly, a teacher in one of your classes may feel that it's okay that 30% of his or her students fail. It's not something the teacher wants, but he or she may be unwilling to make any further changes to him- or herself to help more students pass. That's a mediocre state too. You, yourself, may do homework only about 80% of the time and may have no interest in doing more; that's mediocre too. In this mediocre state, change is absolutely possible. Things could be better! However, for any reason, no change is desired. Often, when people are in this state, you'll hear them say things like, "We're okay doing what we are doing," and "There's no need for change."

Think about aspects of your school where improvement is possible but no one is willing to make a change. For example, do you see the lunch line as a place of perfect human behavior? Are people willing to change to make the lunch line function properly? (As a side note, if you have a perfectly functioning lunch line with no cutting or chaos, please send us a photo on Facebook so you can be recognized for your achievement.) What about in your own life? Are there areas in which you do not feel that you are willing to make a change, even though it's needed and possible? For example, do you feel you are *willing* and *able* to do everything to make your academic situation improve? If you are unwilling but able, that's a mediocre state.

World's Greatest is defined as **change possible, changes wanted, and changes made each day**. It's the ultimate state. There's an old saying, often uttered between adults and younger individuals, "No one expects you to be perfect." Likewise, being World's Greatest has nothing to do with perfection. Instead, it's about being able to improve, wanting to improve, and doing something each day to work toward improvement. Imagine for a moment that you see an individual at your school who you know for a fact is failing out of many of his or her classes. You see this individual in the library, perhaps to quite your surprise, opening his or her textbook for the first time in quite a while and doing the little work that he or she can to improve. No matter if that person's improvement is HUGE or it's just a little, isn't that something to be admired? Isn't any effort to improve one's situation something "greater" than the day before? World's Greatest does not mean "best of the best." Instead, World's Greatest simply means that change was possible, change was wanted, and that some change (regardless of how small) was made for the better.

Have you had an argument or negative interaction with another human being lately? Do you feel that if something like that happened again, you could improve, even in a small way of communicating better? More patiently? Listening better? Being a better family member or friend? Even if the other person in such a conversation was completely wrong, could you have handled it better? Would you be willing to make any small change to make the situation better? If you were to, in fact, make any small change to help any future situations such as these have a better outcome, then you are operating in a World's Greatest state. Likewise, if a school lost twenty students last year as dropouts and the school was willing and able to make changes to help more students stay in school – and the school was actually doing a little work (or more) each day to make that happen – that's World's Greatest too.

One of our dearest friends in Northern California has a HUGE banner hanging in the main foyer of her high school that says, "Through these halls walk the World's Greatest Students." It's not that the students there are perfect. Instead, many can change, many want to change, and many are taking small steps every day to make changes. That's World's Greatest.

In the end, the Three States are not meant to label people or places for labeling's sake. Never would I walk up to someone and say, "Hey, dude, you're mediocre!" Instead, by being able to recognize these Three States, you are more able to help yourself and others move up from No Hope, to Mediocre, to World's Greatest. It's about helping yourself and others, not labeling them.

Three Types of Schools

After learning about the Four C's and the Three States, you're ready to begin applying these to your school. Again, it's not about labeling your school, putting up a banner, shaming others, and praising some. This is about you putting on leader eyes. This is about you seeing how your school is doing in these areas such that you can improve them.

You have a major choice to make as you begin to examine your own school. Do you remember a time when someone said something about you that was true but was quite insulting, frustrating, or angering? The person who said this to you was telling the truth, perhaps. However, this person was not saying it to you in a way that served you. Most people have had the experience of someone trying to help them do better at their homework, because more homework needs to be done. Some healthy ways of helping someone do more homework could include talking with him or her calmly about the possibility of improvement. You could organize tutoring help or study time. You could help the person with the homework yourself. What's not helpful is calling a person "lazy" because of his or her homework issues and then doing nothing about it. That's the kind of choice that you have: Are you going to be a labeler or a leader? A leader recognizes a need and gives others exactly what they need to help them make a change for the better. In the language we have been discussing above, you can choose to recognize what is happening at your school and help your school move to a state of World's Greatest. You do this by being your personal best and by helping others do the same.

Let's look at the Three States and apply them to schools. What might a school in each of the Three States look like?

No Hope High School

At **No Hope High School**, things are going so badly because **people do not want to change** and, accordingly, **change is not possible** (or at least is highly unlikely). When you walk through such a school, it's a place where each person is fighting for his or her survival. Sometimes, it's absolutely obvious from the parking lot that you are walking into a school of this type. It's the type of school where the place and many of the people are severely depressed, violent, and/or apathetic. People at this type of school say, "We don't have time to change, because we're fighting to survive." When outsiders come into such a school and try to help change happen, many will say, "We can't change; you don't know our school." Here is how the Four C's look for such a school:

Cause. An individual's beliefs may include "I can't change," "I'm alone in this," "I don't matter," "I don't want to change," "I don't deserve to matter," "I don't have a future," "Teachers can't help me," "Nothing can change," "No one will listen," "I don't need to change," and "I am a failure."

Command. An individual's actions may include no action, survival actions only, negative or hopeless words, fewer and fewer actions taken, declining physical or academic performance, absence, and self-focused violence.

Conversation. The group's actions may include no action; conflicting actions resulting in declining physical or academic performance, absence, and violence; violence for violence's sake; bullying; negative or hopeless words; and negative words about the school voiced by many.

Culture. The group's beliefs may include "We can't change," "We have to fight for ourselves or our group," "We don't matter," "They don't matter," "We don't want to change," "We don't deserve to matter," "We don't have a future," "Teachers can't help us," "Nothing can change for us," "No one will listen to us," "We don't need to change," "People who tell us that we need to change don't understand our challenges," and "We are failures."

The result of such a school, beyond the evidence listed above, is that everyone connected to this school is harmed. Conditions at such a school can only decline until beliefs and actions change, beginning with one individual and spreading to others. Improving such a place begins with a single person deciding to, first, change him- or herself. Then, that person can help others do the same. No Hope High School could hang a sign above its main entrance that reads, "You don't understand our challenges."

Mediocre High

Mediocre High is a place where **people can change, but they don't want to**. Largely, since many people at Mediocre High believe that things are going "okay" and they are fine with okay, there is no reason for improvements to occur. Here, you'll often find a small group of people who are widely benefited by this place. For example, the most popular students may be treated really well, while everyone else is treated much more poorly (if not ignored entirely). It's the type of place where most people are surviving, but few are thriving. In fact, suggest to individuals of Mediocre High that changes should be made to help more people thrive, and you'll probably hear many objections about why this should or could not happen. People at such a school say things like, "We're doing fine," "We met the minimum requirements," "Most students do okay here," and "We don't need to change." Sometimes, people at such a school, especially when feeling pressure to change, may say, "We'll look into that," "We'll see," and "We'll get a committee going to look in on that." For such a school, change is unlikely because no one really wants to change. Changes, especially fast changes, threaten the feeling of "okay" here. However, change is most definitely possible. Here's what the Four C's look like for this school:

Cause. An individual's beliefs may include "I'm doing fine," "I don't need to improve," "I don't need to concern myself with the future," "I'll work as hard as required to get by," "I just want to get by and be okay," "I'm not any better at any skill than anyone else," "I don't need to work hard," and "Being too ambitious makes other people uncomfortable."

Command. An individual's actions may include minimal action; required actions only; stagnant, unimproved physical or academic performance; words advocating keeping the status quo; obedience to meaningless and unfair policies; using "tradition" as a way of stopping change; and doing nothing to improve where improvement would benefit the individual's life or world around him or her.

Conversation. The group's actions may include minimal action; required actions only; minimal actions resulting in stagnant, unimproved physical or academic performance; allowing for some absence and violence; addressing bullying only after it happens; words discouraging people from improving or changing for the better; and correcting problems only after they occur.

Culture. The group's beliefs may include "There will always be students who don't do well," "It's okay to be okay," "We don't need to be the best," "Helping all students is impossible," "We're just following the rules," "It's not our fault if they don't succeed," "Chill out," "Calm down," "Don't make a fuss," "Slow down," "We'll look into it," "We don't need to all be working for the same purpose," "Not every student has a future," "Some people are talented – others aren't," "We'll get by just fine," and "The purpose of this place is to meet the requirements."

The result of being part of such a school is that while some people succeed, many people do not. People are far less likely to thrive, because it's far more popular to do just enough to be okay and get by. Accordingly, groups of "haves" and "have-nots" exist in this school. There are entire groups of individuals who are barely surviving, while another group is getting resources, attention, and care. What often results is apathy and boredom – sometimes worse. Most of this school's energy is put into making sure problems don't appear. The sign above the entrance to this type of school could read, "We're okay with being okay." This brings us to the final type of school.

World's Greatest High School

The **World's Greatest High School** is a place **where everyone is becoming the best versions of themselves each day**. Here, change is possible, changes are wanted, and changes are made each day. Nearly without exception, every person inside the World's Greatest High School is attempting to become one step better than the day before – that is, they are being their personal best. Even in the case where a person is not purposely improving, others are helping this individual explore the potential for improvement. At such a school, satisfaction comes in getting better and better conditions for more and more individuals, including oneself. People at this school may not be the best in the world, but they are doing what they can today to be better than yesterday. These people say things such as, "I will do better today than I did yesterday," "I'm getting better and better each day," "I will help one more individual today," and "I will work hard to be my personal best." Here, at the World's Greatest High School, "every day is an opportunity to become the World's Greatest Me." This school has a distinct personality. Here's what the Four C's look like for this school:

Cause. An individual's beliefs may include "I am what I believe," "I have a future," "All students have futures," "I can't get anywhere without a teacher," "No one can get anywhere without a teacher," "I am gifted and talented," "All students are gifted and talented," and "Every day is an opportunity to become the World's Greatest Me."

Command. An individual's actions may include improving action, more than required actions, improving physical and academic performance, words advocating for self and others to improve, doing things that improve life, and improving the individual's life or world around him or her.

Conversation. The group's actions may include improving action by all the group members, more than required actions by the group, improving physical and academic performance of the group, words advocating for the group to improve, doing things that improve the life of the group, and improving the lives of others outside the group.

Culture. The group's beliefs may include "We are what we believe – what we believe unifies us," "All students have futures," "No one gets anywhere without a teacher," "All students are gifted and talented," "Every day is an opportunity to become the World's Greatest Me," and "Everything we do, we do with PRIDE."

The result of being in such a school is that each person is encouraged and enabled to become his or her personal best each day. Because students, educators, and parents alike believe that students can do better each day and are willing to take action to make this happen, students do better and better. Because each individual and group within the school has values that support these goals for students, and because each individual and group takes actions toward these ends, students are more able, each day, to explore their greatness. The sign above such a school could read, "Through these halls walk the World's Greatest Students."

Of what type of school would you like to be part? Where do you estimate your current school fits within these types? Are you willing to do the hard work to change that?

Chris

When Chris awoke, he awoke to World's Greatest doctors, family, and friends who were ready to support him. As his mind finally regained consciousness after many weeks of being in a coma, he found himself in unfamiliar, scary surroundings – a place where the outcome was not clear and his well-being was not guaranteed. However, those doctors, family members, and friends to whom he woke up would do anything and everything in their power to ensure that he would become more and more well each day.

Each person believed that Chris could be well and that he or she could help Chris in some way. Chris believed in these people. He trusted them. He believed that he was worth fighting for.

Each person took actions to improve Chris's health and well-being. Each was doing the maximum that he or she possibly could toward Chris's benefit. Chris was doing what he could to improve himself, learning to work his new body in this new situation.

Together, the doctors, family, friends, and Chris were taking actions to further Chris's well-being. They were working as a team for the benefit of Chris.

Together, they were unified by their belief in Chris. They believed Chris had a future. They believed that Chris could not get anywhere without their help at this critical time. They believed that Chris was worth their help. They believed that every day was a chance for them to be the World's Greatest doctor, family member, friend, or man in recovery. Together, they were working to make Chris better.

Like Chris, you are entering a new chapter of your life. Do you believe in yourself? Do you think you're worth being better and better each day? Will you be part of a team that believes these things too and takes action to help you become your World's Greatest Me each day? **Don't your peers deserve the same respect?** Regardless of where you are reading this right now, change is possible. You, your classmates, and your teachers could build the World's Greatest High School right under your feet. The choice is yours. The work that follows that choice will be the greatest challenge.

BLUEPRINT QUESTIONS:

1. Pick one of your classes. Are you working in that class in a No Hope way? Mediocre? World's Greatest? How do you know? What is the evidence of that?

2. In which one of the Three States does your school seem to be operating? How do you know? What is the evidence of that?

3. What is your cause? What do you believe about yourself and others?

4. What in your command is going well? What are you doing that is improving? What would you like to improve?

5. What conversation is going well at your school? What are you doing together that is improving? What would you like to improve?

6. What is the culture of your school? What do people believe together?

DARES:

1. Participate in a group discussion with other student leaders. In what ways is your school like

No Hope High School? Mediocre High? The World's Greatest High School?

2. As a student leadership team, choose one thing that you will do better today than yesterday. Do it.

3. Choose one way you can make the life of another human being better than yesterday. Do it.

CHAPTER THREE

THE WORLD'S GREATEST STUDENT LEADER

"World's Greatest Student Leader is a student who works daily to become his or her personal best and helps others do the same"

How do you feel when you go to school each morning? Do you wake up with a jolt, your legs anxious to start moving toward the door, down the street, and into your school gates? Do you feel your heart pumping in your chest as you enter your first classroom of the day? Do you, inside yourself, feel that "today" may be the best day that you'll ever have so far? Do you experience the teacher's lesson as if this thing, this one thing that he or she is attempting to communicate to you, may be one thing that helps your life become better? Do you look forward to all of this? Why or why not?

Places have a physical and emotional relationship to us. Physically, a place can produce sensations – sights, sounds, smells, touches, tastes – that can produce a variety of reactions within us. Emotionally, a place often draws forward a variety of feelings – excitement, anxiousness, comfort, discomfort, etc. – and each place often has a general feeling that we can ascribe to it. For example, considering an amusement park, what sorts of physical sensations would you experience if you were there now? You may see the lights of the various rides dancing in midair. You may hear the joyful screams of riders. You may smell popcorn, baking cookies, and cotton candy. You may feel the sticky pavement below your feet. You may taste the sugary or salty air on your tongue. What sorts of emotions do you experience in relationship to this place? You may experience excitement. You may experience anxiousness (perhaps roller coasters are not something you enjoy). You may experience joy. At the world's best places, these physical and emotional experiences are not an accident; they are intentionally produced to create an effect.

Think about the best party or celebration that you've ever attended. Seriously, stop and think about it. What was it like there? What sorts of physical sensations were part of this event? Think: sights, sounds, smells, touches, tastes. Stay there in your mind for a moment. What sorts of emotions did you feel in relationship to this event? In your heart, body, and mind, what did you feel because you were part of this thing?

If you had an opportunity to go back there or repeat this event, would you?

Likewise, think of the opposite scenario: Have you been to a celebration or party at which you did not enjoy yourself? What sorts of physical sensations did you experience there? Emotions? If you had the chance to go back, would you?

Naturally, if we were to give you two choices...

#1 – Attend a great event every day, or

#2 – Attend a mediocre or horrible event every day,

which event would you choose to attend? Of course, you would choose to attend the first event. You always would! No person in his or her right mind would sign up to attend anything but the great event – especially when attending the mediocre or horrible event would cause one physical or emotional harm.

Sadly, every single day, you are asking many of your fellow students to attend event #2. You're asking them to attend every single day. You're asking them to be part of something that, in the least, won't do much for them or, at worst, actually causes them great harm. How could it be that a school and the people who run it (including you, being a student leader) would create such a mediocre or horrible daily event and wonder why people are not functioning at their best? This is like cooking bad food and then punishing someone for not liking it or wanting to kick them outside when the food makes them sick.

This Place You Call School

At your school, there are haves, have-nots, and want-nots. There are a group of students who are the celebrities of your school who are, time and time again, recognized through positive time, attention, involvement, and public display. On a daily basis, verbally and silently they are told, "You are wanted here. You are significant." There are a group of students who are constantly receiving repeated, discipline-related time, attention, involvement, and public display. While many who work with these students would say, "If these students would simply clean up their act, they would do well here," the students who experience this on a daily basis hear, loud and clear, "You are not wanted here; this place is not for you." Likewise, there is a group of students, perhaps in the middle, who don't get much attention at all. Because they are not excelling by the school's narrow definition of success and they are not causing sufficient problems to receive discipline, they are caught in the silent no man's land that camouflages them into a space of lonely anonymity. That lonely way of being at school whispers to them daily, "You are not significant."

Take a moment to take stock of your school and its way of working with human beings. Who are the celebrities who are, time and time again, receiving the positive attention of teachers, administrators, other students, and beyond? How is attention shown to these individuals? Who are those who are in trouble time and time again? How is attention shown to these students? What about everyone else? In what ways are many others simply not recognized at all?

At your school, there is a system of upper and lower recognition, where the accomplishments of one group are not celebrated in the same ways as those of others. For example, if your varsity football team won the state championship, a parade may be thrown. A huge party in the middle of your school may be organized. Word would hit the front pages, perhaps, of your local newspaper. Hundreds of people would be involved in this celebration. Conversely, if your varsity girls soccer team won the state championship, would the celebration be as vigorous? Would the outpouring of excitement, support, and attention be of the same caliber? Even if your school already has aspired to be World's Greatest, there are still individuals, groups, teams, clubs, and many others who simply get lost in between the haves and the want-nots. Chances are, your school is like most: some are recognized; many are not.

To further understand your school, let's consider the following groups. Then we'll discuss what you, as a student leader, can do to help.

The Royal Family

The **Royal Family** consists of the celebrities of your school. These are the individuals who are positively recognized and celebrated on a regular basis. These are the "popular" kids. These students hang out in many places, but, it so happens, you often find them in school leadership, varsity sports, on the stage, in the rally, holding the trophy, or getting that certificate. You know a person is a member of the Royal Family when you know that person because you've heard or seen him or her being celebrated, rewarded, or applauded before – even if you've never personally spoken to him or her. You may know the person because you are part of the same Royal Family! The Royal Family is at the heart of the power structures of Mediocre High and No Hope High School. Members of the Royal Family are often in positions of power in such schools and use these positions to ensure that they are continually celebrated and that their friends are treated similarly. The result of this is a clique-based system of being on campus – you are either "in" the popular group or you are not.

Think about your last school celebration. Do you believe that there were many different groups of individuals from many different walks of life being celebrated? Or, like many schools, were the athletes the sole recipients of the celebration? Alternatively, was it the student leaders who were the primary focus? Or were the student leaders making many others the emphasis of attention? Even within the class in which you sit right now, is there a group of students (such as the oldest students) who have all the power, while the rest of the students have less and less depending on age or popularity? When there is a system of a small group of individuals who are celebrated while the largest group of others are not, most students feel that they are not included; they often feel like they are living school life as spectators. After all, if you have 1,000 students and only 100 of them are celebrated at the rally, you can't say there is no preferential treatment.

Kileys and Alyssas

Kileys and **Alyssas** are those students who need extra support to survive and thrive. Park's twin granddaughters were born unexpectedly and early. When Kiley and Alyssa's mother went into labor in the early morning, Park was scheduled to speak to several hundred leadership students that same day. I remember standing there in the parking lot of the speaking venue with him: He looked quite tired – he was a dad who was worried for his daughter and his granddaughters. Honestly, I did not expect him to show up to the event that day – but there was nothing that he could do at the hospital. The only thing he knew for sure was that many, many junior high and high school students were expecting him to speak. When he walked out onto the stage that morning, he did not stick to the script of his talk. Instead, rather than talking about the Royal Family or student leaders, he talked about his granddaughters. Kiley and Alyssa needed lots of help to enter this world. They needed help after they arrived. Nothing about their arrival was routine. Their presence was not easy; they were experiencing challenges simply to breathe. However, the doctors did not send them away. The doctors did not punish the twins for their lack of ability to survive on their own. Of course, the doctors did whatever was needed to help those kids survive and thrive. The point Park made to those many leadership students that morning holds much truth: There are Kileys and Alyssas on your campus. There are students who need your support. They can't make it on their own. Will you ignore them or get angry because they can't make it without you? Or will you rise up to give those students that which is needed for them to survive and thrive? Like Kiley and Alyssa (that morning), there are students on your campus today who are on life support. Will you pull the plug on them? Or will you give them your personal best so they can grow?

The Kileys and Alyssas of your school come in many forms. Basically, these students are those who will not survive the junior high or high school environment unless they receive the support they need. Without help, they won't pass many classes. They may drop out without your help. They may be the target of violence or bullying unless they are protected. These students can't handle being left alone like so many students are on your campus. They don't need the support that most students get – they need much more. They need you. Why would you not give them what they need?

Austins

Austins are advanced students. Park's grandson (he likes to talk about his grandchildren) was born eleven pounds twelve ounces (most babies are born around seven pounds), already fitting into three-month clothes. He's a big boy. No extra support, beyond what was expected, was required. Similarly, the Austins of your school are in the advanced and honors classes. They are the students who work hard for their grades but don't necessarily struggle to achieve them. These students do well without the intervention of adults. They do what's required. They are often recognized for having the best grades. These are often the best kind of students to have in a group doing a project. They are good at getting things done. Often, without much support, they are able to excel academically. These are your honor roll students. These are your students who get scholarships and get high scores on college entrance exams.

Consider the Austins of your campus. What sorts of challenges do they face daily? Though these students may make getting good grades look easy, how is it hard to be an Austin? Often, the challenge of being an advanced student is to continue performing at this level for a long period of time. Further, Austins have significant gifts, talents, and skills beyond those that are academic, and sometimes these are ignored. Austins may be working hard to receive high marks in their language arts and math classes, having to sacrifice time in the athletics and the arts. Further, the pressure can be quite intense, with many people watching them, expecting them to get the highest grades, attend the best universities, and be the academic leaders of the school. Right or wrong, in the end, the goal of most schools is to turn all students into Austins – even if students are not fully able to make that transformation.

The Austins of your school need your help as well. They need your help to take time to enjoy the social aspects of school. They need your help to explore their gifts and talents outside of academics. They need your help so that they can be part of the support system that helps other students around them grow as human beings. They need your help to step from being a leader of themselves into being, also, a leader of others. Without your leadership, they can't become the best leaders that they can be. It can be quite easy to ignore this group, because they may already get significant recognition on campus. However, they need you to help them become, more and more, leaders who help others around them.

Camo Kids

So far, we've mentioned the advanced students (the Austins), the students who need extra support (the Kileys and Alyssas), and the celebrities at your school (the Royal Family). What about all the other students who don't fit into any of these groups? It may not be too hard to imagine: With some students being the celebrities, some being the students who need lots of support, and others being the advanced academic students – what about everyone else? **Camo Kids** are those students who, on a regular basis, do not feel needed or wanted on your school campus. These are the students who show up to your rallies and celebrations, look at the people involved, and say, "This is not an event for me. All I am here for is to be a part of the audience." Imagine that for a second: What would it be like to go days and days at school feeling like you were simply a silent person expected to watch other people be important? The sad thing is, many students at your school feel like this every day.

Camo Kids are the students who do not take part in school activities unless required to do so – there is no reason for them to participate, because they feel that they are not wanted or needed. These are the students who may see your leadership team doing a lunchtime activity, rally, or celebration, and purposely walk around the crowd, avoiding being part of the action. These are the students who sit at your rallies, blank faced, staring or looking at their phones or the ground. They don't pay attention because there is not much reason for them to do so, beyond being spectators. Each day, Camo Kids are asked (and often forced) to be part of activities and school functions that, they believe, do not interest them. They believe that events and moments such as these don't apply to them. They feel apathetic, unneeded, or unwanted. Should you spend time convincing these Camo Kids that they are wrong? No. Rather, create moments for these students that *show them* that they are both needed and wanted.

This is the place that you call school. Inside this school are many types of people, many of whom could fit into one of the categories that we mentioned above. As you read about these, you already may be thinking about ways that you can make the lives of these individuals better on your campus. However, before you actually go out and help these people as a team of student leaders, let's talk about what the ultimate team of student leaders could do. Let's talk about what it would look like to be the best team of student leaders your campus has ever seen. Let's talk about World's Greatest Student Leaders and their team.

World's Greatest Student Leaders

The **World's Greatest Student Leader** is a student who works daily to become his or her personal best and helps others do the same. The World's Greatest Student Leader is not the best student academically, athletically, or artistically. Instead, today, he or she is working to be the best self that he or she has ever been. While one could be working to be the best of oneself five years from now, the World's Greatest Student Leader works simply to be one step better today than yesterday. On top of that, he or she is working to help other students (and adults) do the same. These leaders are not only experts at being "one step better" themselves; they are also masters of helping other people on their campus and beyond become one step better too.

When you look at the World's Greatest Student Leader, you see an individual who is concerned with outdoing him- or herself. This individual may or may not have huge goals for his or her life after high school. What concerns this person most, however, is today: being "the best me that I can be." By this standard, such a student leader can be a member of the Royal Family, a Kiley or Alyssa, an Austin, or a Camo Kid, but what makes this individual the World's Greatest Student Leader is (1) working each day to be one step better and (2) helping others do the same thing. Think about yourself. Are you working (truly working) to be better today than yesterday? Alternatively, are you simply trying to do just as well as yesterday? Are you working to help others become their personal best? Or, simply, are you allowing others to be as they are without any help at all?

With so many ideas about what defines a "student leader," what sets the World's Greatest Student Leader apart is his or her tenacity to operate at his or her personal best. Because of this, you will see a World's Greatest Student Leader engaging in three behaviors at your school. As you are reading about these, assess yourself. Are you doing this? The World's Greatest Student Leader...

Teaches the Culture

The first behavior of the World's Greatest Student Leader is that he or she **teaches the culture**. Imagine, for a moment, that you are a new student on your campus. It's your first day. You walk into school, you get your schedule, you go to your first class, second, third, and so on. You go to lunch. You go to a few more classes, and you go home. During that time during your first day as a student here, what sorts of lessons did you learn about your school? What did you learn about your fellow students, your teachers, your community, your lunch line, your food, or your traditions? It's not that you learned nothing! In fact, you probably learned much simply by watching. What sorts of lessons about your school would any new student learn on his or her first day? Are these the lessons that you want these students to receive? Consider taking your next school day to put on the eyeballs of a brand new student and ask yourself some questions:

What did I learn when I was driving up to the front of my school?

What did I learn as I was walking through the gates?

What did I learn as I went to get my schedule or find out the location of my first class?

What did I learn about my school and my peers in the hallways?

What about the classrooms? What did I learn about my teachers and peers there?

What did I learn about meal times, lines, and bathrooms?

What did I learn about the food?

What did I learn about the traditions, celebrations, or rituals of the school?

What did I learn about my place within this school?

Do I feel like this is the kind of place for me? How do I know?

What did I learn about how people are treated here? Is this a place of trust? Kindness?

The World's Greatest Student Leader does not leave any of the answers to these questions to chance. Instead, such a leader purposefully teaches the culture of the school to newcomers. Further, even for those who have been at the school for some time, a World's Greatest Student Leader continually reminds and reteaches the culture to the people within the school. Such a student leader would know, from the moment that a new student arrived on campus, that his or her job was to teach that newcomer about the culture of the school. This student leader would communicate to this student what type of place this was – and that the school is so fortunate to have the new student there! If a World's Greatest Student Leader does not teach the culture, someone will. Someone will always be there to teach the culture: Someone could teach your newcomers that this school is a horrible place. Someone could teach your newcomers that this is not the place for them. Someone could teach your newcomers (or the rest of your fellow students, for that matter) that your school is run down, unwelcoming, dangerous, and not the type of place that has any sorts of opportunities for growth at all. Remember: If you do not teach the culture of your school, someone will. The World's Greatest Student Leader teaches the culture such that more students can be enabled to be the best versions of themselves: a culture of significance where everyone matters. The greatest way to teach this culture is not through words – it's through action.

Creates Rose Petal Moments

The second behavior of the World's Greatest Student Leader is that he or she **creates Rose Petal Moments**. As discussed in the introduction to this book, Rose Petal Moments are moments where people get to experience significance. When you think about the Royal Family of your school, it's easy to see that these individuals continually feel significant and wanted: they are the celebrities after all. However, what about everyone else? Are there times regularly, throughout the year, that each and every single person on your campus feels that he or she is significant, wanted, needed, and appreciated? So easy would it be to say, "Well, we had a rally last semester, and we showed off every athletic team on campus! They all walked through a tunnel!" Meanwhile, the rest of the students of the school were forced to watch with no recognition at all. If you were to go to a board in your classroom and write out the names of every single official and unofficial group from your school and were to draw an "X" through those that you celebrated within the last month, what would you find? Chances are, if you are like most student leadership teams, it would become clear that you tend to celebrate a handful of groups fairly regularly, while others may be lucky to receive more than a single moment of recognition the entire year. Ask yourself, "Would I go to a restaurant where I was only personally served one out of 180 times I visited?" Are you, then, surprised when students don't feel like they are being recognized when they will only be recognized (maybe) one out of 180 school days each year? Without purposely creating Rose Petal Moments for the fellow inhabitants of your school, can you see how you are simply asking the majority of students to just sit and watch while other people are celebrated? Chances are, you, yourself, would not want to be one of these individuals being forced to watch other people matter. There is an alternative.

The World's Greatest Student Leader is an architect of Rose Petal Moments for both his or her fellow students and the adults on campus. Such a leader is an expert at seeing how small moments of significance can have a lifelong impact. There are people on your campus today who will not hear their names said verbally by anyone. They will go more than twenty-four hours without anyone even saying their name. What impact, then, would simply your eye contact, a "hello," and the utterance of their name have on them? It would mean the world! Consider, then, how much more impactful a planned moment of significance could be. Writing a few sentences on a 3" x 5" notecard of why you appreciate this person would mean even more. How impactful could a lunch invitation ("Hey! Would you eat over here with us?") be to such a person? The fact is, though, many students are not unlike this nameless person each day. So many walk around campus during lunch, not stopping for an instance because it would prove that they do not have anyone with whom to eat. So many students spend the opening moments of their day before their first class looking for others whom they call friend. What, then, would it mean for you, or anyone else for that matter, to have just one person do something out of the ordinary for you – regardless of how small that gesture of kindness? The World's Greatest Student Leader is a master at recognizing moments such as these and building them. Creating one of these is as simple as saying "hello." It can be as grand and complicated as creating an amazing graduation ceremony. It could be any moment of significance in between that makes another human being feel significant. As the World's Greatest Student Leader, you will learn that you have immense power over the thoughts and emotions of other human beings. With a single look, you can mean the world to a person. With a single word, you can give someone life (or perhaps save it). And you could give that to someone else. That's power!

Develops the World's Greatest in Team and Others
The final behavior of the World's Greatest Student

Leader is that he or she **develops the "World's Greatest" in his or her team and others**. The World's Greatest quality is simply being one step better than the day before. It doesn't mean that one is becoming the best of the best. It means that one is becoming one's personal best. There are individuals at your school who may call themselves "leaders" but regularly make it their business to tear others down. Instead of making it part of their daily life to make other people around them more and more powerful, they spend great amounts of energy keeping other people powerless, helpless, and with little chance of getting out. This, by far, is the worst form of leadership (if you can even call it that): where a person is so threatened by others that he or she seeks to harm or, at least, keep people without a chance of having further power. So often within a student leadership team, there is a Royal Family that holds all the power and works quite hard to ensure the Kileys, Alyssas, and Camo Kids don't have a chance to be in a place of further leadership. Truly, this is the exact opposite of the behavior of the World's Greatest Student Leader.

The World's Greatest Student Leader develops the World's Greatest qualities of his or her team and those around them. Wherever there is a group of haves and have-nots, the World's Greatest Student Leader works to make sure that everyone has the chance to live more and more as their personal best each day. Instead of being threatened by the advancement of other students and members of his or her team, this student leader works to help others do better and better – even if that means that such a leader must give up his or her power for another to become his or her personal best. Rather than the youngest students being in service to the older students, the older students are supporting the younger ones so that these students may, one day, be the top leaders.

The World's Greatest Student Leadership Team

The World's Greatest Student Leadership Team, therefore, is a group of World's Greatest Student Leaders who, together, teach the culture, create Rose Petal Moments, and develop the World's Greatest in their team and others at their school. This is not your everyday student leadership team whose purpose is to throw rallies and paint posters. This group is playing an enthralling game: the game of helping each and every single person on campus become his or her personal best one day at a time, one interaction at a time. While everyday student leadership teams will set huge lofty goals for the next ten months, only to ignore these when they get busy and overwhelmed by the school year's end, the World's Greatest Student Leadership Team makes it their moment-by-moment *practice* to give every person they can the conditions for a more thriving life. Consider what would have more impact upon you if you were a student athlete competing later this week: a poster saying, "Go [insert your school name here]!" or, alternatively, a poster that says, "Go [your name here]!" along with a quote about why you love to play this sport (because a member of the World's Greatest Student Leadership Team came to you and interviewed you last week). Also consider what would have more of an impact upon you: a hundred posters saying, "Welcome to [insert your school name here]!" or one handwritten 3" x 5" note card from a student you've met before saying that he or she is excited that you are at your school. Most importantly, would it not be most impactful for another human being on campus to know who you are and how you are trying to be the best "me" this week, and be there to help you (even in the smallest of ways) do that?

So, you can only be the World's Greatest Student Leadership Team when each and every person in your group is working to become the best version of him- or herself and is taking the three actions above to help others do the same. Thinking back to the Four C's, let's take a moment to look at the specifics of how the World's Greatest Student Leadership Team members think and act by themselves and with the rest of their team.

Cause

Specifically, a World's Greatest Student Leadership Team member believes in the six World's Greatest Values. **The World's Greatest Values** are **six values held by a person seeking to become his or her World's Greatest Me**. These values are the personal tenets or beliefs that guide the actions of this individual in service of him or her being his or her personal best. If you look at some of the happiest and most successful persons in your life, you may see these ways of thinking alive within them. To serve you, through the course of this book we will be offering you these ways of seeing your world along with detailed discussions about what they are and how you can apply them. However, in brief, here are **The World's Greatest Values**:

Value #1. We are what we believe – what we believe unifies us. At the World's Greatest High School, my beliefs greatly influence how I go about my work, and our beliefs greatly influence how we go about our work together.

Value #2. All kids have futures. At the World's Greatest High School, we know that every student has a future and that we have the ability to greatly impact that future.

Value #3. No one gets anywhere without a teacher. At the World's Greatest High School, we recognize that no one gets anywhere without a teacher and that the impact of teachers is exponential.

Value #4. All students are gifted and talented. At the World's Greatest High School, we seek out and celebrate the gifts, talents, and skills that each person brings into the school.

Value #5. Every day is an opportunity to become the World's Greatest Me. At the World's Greatest High School, each person on campus seeks to be a better version of "me" than the day before – "my personal best." The members of the World's Greatest High School work purposefully to develop each person's gifts, talents, and skills.

Value #6. Everything we do, we do with PRIDE. At the World's Greatest High School, the school's one-of-a-kind culture of "Greatness" is clear in everything it does.

These are The World's Greatest Values. This way of thinking has a huge impact upon the beliefs and values of a World's Greatest Student Leadership Team member. Because this team member believes that each and every single person on campus has a future, he or she believes that helping out these individuals is worthwhile. Because such a student leader believes that helping others is worthwhile, he or she believes that it's possible to be of service. The World's Greatest Student Leadership Team member thinks, "I have a future. They have a future. Because we have a future, we can help one another get to that future."

Command

Since the World's Greatest Student Leadership Team member believes that he or she has a future and others have a future too, and because he or she values helping others take steps toward this future, this team member behaves in ways that support these values. Accordingly, the focus of this type of student leader is that he or she is trying to be his or her personal best each day – one step better than yesterday. Think about something about yesterday that could be improved today. The World's Greatest Student Leader will work today to improve, even if the gains are small. This is not limited to just one item per day. Many World's Greatest Student Leaders can be bettering themselves in a whole host of ways in a single day. So, in short, each World's Greatest Student Leadership Team member's actions show him or her working to be his or her personal best.

Conversation

Together, the entire World's Greatest Student

Leadership Team behaves in ways that support all the people on the campus in becoming their personal best. Together, they work with one another to become the best versions of themselves within their team. They work together to be the best team they can be. They work with the team to help others, outside the team, become the best versions of themselves as well. Rather than the focus being upon throwing dances for the purpose of entertainment, they throw dances to support each guest in becoming his or her best self. Rather than entertainment for entertainment's sake, it's an entertaining, meaningful celebration for the sake of growing and enriching human beings.

Culture

The World's Greatest Student Leadership Team collectively believes in the six World's Greatest Values. Simply put, the World's Greatest Student Leadership Team, together, believes that each person on campus has a future. This belief leads these leaders to understand that they have significant power in being able to help others make or break that future. They see that by helping others take steps today to be better human beings, they can nurture that future and bring it into being. Alternatively, this student leadership team understands that if they are not careful and attentive, they could seriously damage or destroy the potential for those futures. Your World's Greatest Student Leadership Team must understand that your belief in the people you serve is chief among all things. You must see that the people you serve not only need you but inherently deserve your service as well. This is not a club or hobby you've joined; you're going to actually save people's lives.

It Starts With You

The team, however, is secondary to you. You, first, must take the steps needed each day to be better than yesterday. You must believe and behave in such a way that betters your life and seeks to better the lives of others. Until you are personally able to do that, you can't be part of a team that is trying to do that. After all, if you are on a basketball team, it would make no sense for you to get out onto the court and try to play tennis. Imagine if Chris woke up to a group of doctors who were *not* committed to him surviving and being as well as possible? What if Chris awoke to lazy doctors and medical staff who were just doing the minimum to get by? What if you could be doing that same thing to your fellow students around you? They may need you to be your personal best in a moment of great need – not an "okay" version of you who is just looking to get by easily. How are you being less than what is needed by those around you in their great times of need? If you truly want to be part of the World's Greatest Student Leadership Team, you have to commit and take action to become the "World's Greatest Me": your personal best. There cannot be a World's Greatest Student Leadership Team without a World's Greatest Me. It starts with you.

BLUEPRINT QUESTIONS:

---

1. Describe a positive event in your life that holds great meaning to you. What sights, sounds, smells, tastes, and touches occurred during this event?

2. Describe a day in the life of being at your school. What do you see, hear, smell, taste, and feel throughout each hour of your day?

3. Who are a group of "haves" on your campus? Who are a group of "have-nots" on your campus? Why are these groups haves or have-nots? What do they have? What do they not have?

4. Compare and contrast what a school day is like for one student in each of the following groups: the Royal Family, Kileys and Alyssas, Austins, and Camo Kids.

5. What Rose Petal Moments have you witnessed for each of the groups mentioned above?

DARES:

---

1. As a student leadership class, make a list of all the groups on your campus. Put a checkmark by each group if you have celebrated them in the last 30 days. Notice who received celebration and recognition and those who did not. Discuss this with your team.

2. As a student leadership class, make a list of all the groups on your campus. Put a square around those whom you consider to be the Royal Family. Put a circle around the Kileys and Alyssas. Put a star around the Austins. Look at who is left. Are these the Camo Kids? What about all the others who did not even make it on this list? Who are these individuals? Discuss this with your team. Now, for each of these groups, what Rose Petal Moments can you identify that have taken place this year through your action and direction?

3. On your own, spend one day away from your friends outside of class. Walk a different route into school, around school, and to class than you usually take. Imagine you are a new student. What do you see, smell, hear, taste, and feel throughout your day as a "new student"? Discuss what you discover with your team.

CHAPTER FOUR

EXPLORE YOUR GREATNESS

"Everyday moments of significance will have a profound impact upon who you become."

We have a secret for you – one that we like to tell as many people as possible. Is that still a secret? Either way, here it goes: The most significant moment of your life could happen today. In fact, it could happen right now. Significant moments, the ones that change who you are forever, happen in the everyday life – and, if you're so fortunate, a great one could occur for you today at any moment. In your life, significant moments could happen at any second.

Your high school graduation. Your wedding. Your first new car. Your first amazing payday. Your meeting your lifelong best friend for the first time. These are all moments that most people consider to be some of the greatest potential moments of their lives. When you read stories or watch movies about "big things" happening in people's lives, these are often the moments that come to mind. When you are walking to class, sitting working on an assignment at your desk, or taking the steps to get home each day, these don't feel as if they have the same weight. The general idea is that significant moments in life, the ones that change us forever, usually happen in predefined, planned blips, in this hopefully long timeline we call life. However, we are here to tell you that while many of your most significant moments will happen like that, so many of the instances of life that build us up (or tear us down) as human beings happen in our everyday lives.

Imagine the moment when Chris woke up with enough mental clarity to hear what had transpired to place him in the hospital – and to hear about the state of his body. He was told that he had a "C4" fracture of his spine. He was told that many people with this injury never walk again. He was told that he broke his neck and that he would be lucky to have much movement in his body at all going forward. Placing yourself in Chris's shoes, in even the smallest way, ask yourself, "Would I have the determination and belief in myself to bravely know that life could keep getting better despite these circumstances?" For Chris, he could answer "yes": He had no doubt that he would be fine. He had no doubt that he would exceed the expectations of his doctors. He had no doubt that he would walk again. He had no doubt that he would live a good life – and that he probably would live a great life at that. What allowed Chris to believe this to the degree that he did?

Numerous significant moments over his life had built up this belief in himself. His family's unwavering support for one another allowed him to see that he was not alone. His training in the martial arts and meditation allowed him to see one moment at a time – even in the most frightening of circumstances. His friends, mentors, and acquaintances at school further allowed him to see that better (if not the best) moments of life were still to come. Every moment that contributed to his seeing that he would pull through and live a great life was significant – even if Chris did not realize it along the way.

Everyday moments of significance will have a profound impact upon who you become. Already, you have had hundreds (if not thousands) of instances in your life that were of great significance, for good or for bad. Each of these moments will make you more able or less able to experience the life you desire. While many of these moments will strike you immediately as being of great importance, many of these moments will come to you later in life as the ones that have contributed to or dissuaded you from that which you want most. Consider, for example, the story that opened the introduction of this book. When that young lady arrived on campus to see the giant banner ("Prom?"), teddy bear, and flowers, this was a significant moment in her life. Forever, as long as her mind can, she will remember that young man who had created that moment for her. She will remember the friends and acquaintances who came together to create that moment. She will remember the feeling of surprise, not knowing what was happening until she put all the mental pieces together – this moment was FOR HER. This moment told her she was supported, loved, cared for, and worth it. This moment spoke to her. This moment will continue to speak to her. This moment will keep telling her that she was supported for years to come. Significant moments, regardless of what they are, will continue to speak to you for years to come.

As Chris received words from many doctors, many telling him that he would never walk again, some saying that he would be unlikely to have much movement in his upper body, many of the moments of significance in his life were speaking to him:

"A great life for me is still ahead,"

"I have people around me who love me and will support me,"

"I know that I can carry on,"

"I will get through this," and many others.

Because of the significant moments of Chris's past, he was able to believe that he had a future. For him, he was not on his death bed; he was living another day in his life leading to better and better days.

You are headed toward better days.

You have people around you who love you and will support you.

You can carry on.

You will get through this.

You can explore your greatness today.

As this chapter starts, we invite you to make this a significant moment that will speak to you for years to come.

Explore Your Greatness

When a person is becoming one step better than yesterday and giving his or her personal best, we say that such a person is becoming his or her **World's Greatest Me**. Let's say you, for example, decide that you are going to better yourself today in one area of your life. Perhaps you are going to do one piece of homework that you neglected yesterday, say "hello" to one more person, or spend five more minutes listening carefully to a friend – you could be said to be becoming your World's Greatest Me. This is not to say that you are the greatest person on the planet and that we should have a framed picture of you in every classroom. Instead, being your World's Greatest Me means that you are the best version of yourself that you have seen. You're the best version of yourself because you are better than yesterday – and each day forward you'll be better and better. By exploring your greatness each day, by seeing how you can be better and by taking actual steps to become better, you are stretching yourself further and further into more powerful iterations of this person you call "me" – the "me" that you want to be.

Think about a world-class basketball player. When that person was fourteen years old, he or she did not hit the court for the first time playing like a world-class basketball player. In fact, as much as he or she could have great hopes to be such an amazing player, that person may not have known for sure that he or she would be a player of such magnitude later on. Regardless, day by day, he or she went from a beginner, to a novice, to a better and better player. Each day, this person dedicated him- or herself to becoming a better player by practicing. This person made decisions each day that contributed more and more to his or her becoming a world-class player. He or she probably continued to get better through high school until he or she was drafted into a professional team. Daily, this person explored his or her greatness *today*. Likewise, you can say to yourself, "What is one thing that I could do one step better than yesterday? What of my personal best can I give right now?" If you did that, you could be said to be exploring your greatness just like this athlete. This exploration is the daily stretching of what you have done before into one step better than yesterday. Are you up for such a challenge?

Depending on who you are and where you sit right now, you may have different levels of clarity about your ability to become better and better at whatever you want. It's possible that you feel that you are sitting in a nearly hopeless situation, where getting through the day is a significant challenge. Alternatively, you could feel that things are "okay" and that there is some potential for something better but that it will take lots of energy (perhaps that you don't feel you have) to make any change. Further, you may be in an environment that is pushing and motivating you to be your best. Regardless, the first step in exploring your greatness is a small one. It's microscopic. Anyone can do it. Simply name one thing that you did yesterday; it could be (almost) anything. The next step, then, is quite small too. Do that thing simply one step, one second, one moment, one instance better than yesterday. It's that move to do one thing better than before that can lift you (one step at a time) from where you are toward the destination you desire. For example, you may have a great desire to be more physically fit. Each day, you take the shortest possible path to class. You have a couple extra minutes when you arrive to class each day. So, instead, you decide to take a longer walking route to class today. You have to move faster, so your heart rate goes up. You have to walk farther, so your muscles are having to work. While we don't recommend that you put a sweatband on your head and jog to class, you get the idea: Exploring your greatness starts with seeing where you were yesterday, taking one more step to be better than yesterday, and repeating that each day on and on. Regardless of where you are and what's going on, you can have a better today than yesterday. You can.

However, as much as that sounds easy, it's not always that easy. In your daily life, you will have moments of significance that will make you more able or less able to become "my personal best." There are situations that will speak to you, saying that you can make it, that you are worth it, and that there is a way forward that you are able to take. There are moments, also, that will attempt to convince you that there is no way forward and that nothing good is on the future horizon. Regardless of your best intentions, it can be quite difficult to only listen to the moments that scream,

"You can do it!" Chances are, if you are like most people, the day can be a roller coaster of emotions that does not necessarily encourage you to be your World's Greatest Me. There are moments where you feel lost, tired, bored, and confused. You might feel alone. When that young lady received her prom invitation, there were others who did not feel like they were part of that celebration. Camo Kids like these received the message that it was just another day of not being included – another day that was not designed for them in a place that was hardly made for them at all. In the same instant, one set of individuals felt like they were seen, like they were part of something big, and like they were important, while another group felt lonely, hopeless, and unimportant. How could your daily life be more and more full of relevant, significant moments that were designed to help you further become your World's Greatest Me? For such a possibility, others have to be involved.

The way that you see "you" is not the way that others see you. Our eyes, especially those that look into the mirror, are quite easily deceived by the coloring of our minds. One of our friends, for example, had a favorite shirt, his "party shirt." This shirt, he believed, made him look absolutely amazing. The colors and fit of the t-shirt made him feel like a superstar. Any chance he had to wear that shirt, it was on! When he was a freshman in college, it was the first big celebration of the year at his dorm. He had been imagining for much of his high school life what it would be like to be at university and able to hang out with friends at a celebration of such epic proportions. Out of excitement, on went that party shirt.

He had an amazing night that night with friends – one that he would probably never forget. However, a few weeks later, he and his dorm mates sat down, as was the custom of the time before cell phones with cameras existed (yes, our friend is ancient), and watched a video of the party that someone had taken with a "camcorder." On the television, there was the party! He began to feel quite happy nearly reliving it as he began to re-experience all the memories of that night. Then, his heart became crushed: There he was on video, wearing that shirt. However, much to his surprise, he did not look like he was having the time of his life. He was removed from the crowd, almost as if he was not part of the group. That t-shirt looked horrible, more baggy than he expected, and made him feel quite silly. On the video, he had a look on his face that did not look like he was having fun. "Is this how I looked to people that night?" he thought to himself. He attempted to laugh it off a bit, pointing himself out to the rest of his dorm mates, saying, "Wow! There's me! Looks like you caught me at a bad time with that camera!" Much to his further surprise, a few of his dorm mates remarked, "You're our favorite weirdo; we love keeping you around." This story is an example of how what we see of ourselves each day is not necessarily how others see us. Likewise, what we think about our abilities is not always accurate in our eyes. To become the World's Greatest Me, you're going to have to develop your gifts and talents. To best develop those, you're going to need someone to point out what you don't see. Likewise, for others to develop their gifts and talents, they're going to need your help too. By having others help us see ourselves more clearly and help us develop our gifts and talents, we can turn around and help others do that as well. We call this type of relationship "mentorship."

Mentoring

To sum up this chapter so far, we have presented you with two central ideas. First, you can become your personal best, your World's Greatest Me, by exploring your greatness daily – by becoming one step better than the day before. Second, significant moments in your life can encourage you toward or discourage you from this goal of becoming your personal best. Here, we add a final idea, one that is central to this book and one that is central to your role as a student leader: *You cannot become your World's Greatest Me without the assistance of others*. Simultaneously, others cannot become their personal best without you. When you think about the place that you call school, why does anyone have to be there anyway? We live in a world where you can find out nearly anything from a four-inch screen that is probably sitting in your pocket right now. What prevents you from learning the math skills required by life on your own, today? Well, if you are honest with yourself, it's because you probably would not or could not do this on your own without the help of a mentor. By mentor, we do not mean a wise elderly woman who provides you with coaching while gifting you a cold beverage. Instead, a **mentor**, in the sense we intend, is a supporter – one who assists. A mentor is someone who works to assist you by creating significant moments that will encourage you to further become your personal best. This is what a true student leader is: a mentor who does exactly this. What results is a cycle that supports the mentor and the mentee. It involves receiving and giving. Give others the opportunity to see and develop their gifts. From there, they may help you see more in you than you currently see in yourself.

Receiving

When you surround yourself with mentors who are assisting you in becoming your personal best, you are not alone. People are surrounding you and encouraging you to discover what it is that makes you tick. What is it that you desire in life? What is it that you are, potentially, destined to do? As we've said before, there are gifts and talents you have as an individual, and you can only develop those so far on your own. When you allow others to be part of that process, they're able to stretch you in ways that you potentially would not be able to grow on your own. Like our dear friend with the party shirt, it's possible that you are not able to see the ways in which you can grow. It's possible that the gifts and talents that you have as a human being are not entirely apparent to you. When others are part of the process of you becoming your World's Greatest Me, they can help you uncover those gifts and talents. When you look around you at the students in your student leadership class (if you are in such a thing), it's highly possible that there are many people here who have helped you in some way. Perhaps the teacher of this class has helped you in some way – and by "help," I don't mean he or she has made you the ultimate athlete or has given you a job that provides you with a suitcase of money. However, in some small way, the people around you have made your day better, they have made your life at the school better, they've provided encouragement or inspiration by placing you amidst a group of people like these, and you're better for it. When you place yourself with others and allow them to bless you, you're better for it. You're better for it than you ever could possibly be alone, because you're allowing others to be part of you.

When you allow others to be part of your process, becoming your World's Greatest Me, what develops is a mentor-mentee relationship. These mentors begin to understand a great deal about you. They begin to understand what gifts and talents you have to offer yourself, the school, the community, and the world. They see ways in which you can stretch those gifts and talents to become a better you. Likewise, they see ways in which they can create significant moments that can help support and stretch your gifts, talents, and skills. Because of this, you're better: you stretch, you grow, you're more able to take the daily steps required to become your World's Greatest Me. Because of that, you're more able to help others and yourself. One student, for example, was placed unexpectedly in a student leadership class. She had not planned on being there. She was shy, secretly angry at life, and fairly resentful of nearly everything and everyone. She had lived a very hard life. Three student leaders stepped up and took her under their wings. They recognized that she had an immense talent for speaking in front of others with bravery. In greater and greater ways each day, they provided her with a way to use that talent by being an in-the-hall spokesperson for one of their up-and-coming celebrations, by being a small-group leader, by being the class commissioner, and, one day, even by speaking in front of the entire school in one of the rallies. Because a handful of student leader mentors saw what this young woman was capable of doing, she was able to grow in the gifts and talents that she did not even know were there. By creating significant moments, the mentors enabled her to become her personal best in ways that she never could have on her own.

So, put yourself in situations where you can reap the benefits of being mentored by others. It's not easy being part of a team. It's not easy placing yourself in a situation where you could potentially be hurt. It can feel intimidating to put yourself in situations where things can get messy – where things may not work out in the ways that you expect. However, by placing yourself in the hands of good people, they can encourage you to grow in your gifts and talents. You can advance toward being your personal best. As human beings, we have a huge predisposition toward routine. We tend to do the same things that are comfortable to us over and over again, even when they are not necessarily the best for us. It's like the solo runner who goes to the track every morning for his run. He runs for a year, nearly every day. He's showing up every day, but he's not getting any better than the first few weeks he began running. However, as he arrives to the track early one morning, sitting on the bleachers in the fog is an elderly man. As the young man begins to run, the elderly man begins to yell, "Go faster!" The young man looks at this elderly man with apathy and says to himself, "Why should I listen to this old man yelling at me from inside the fog?" The next day, he comes to the track again, and the old man yells at him, "Run faster! Run faster!" The young man ignores the old man again. Finally, on the third day, he hits the track, and there's the old man again yelling, "Go faster! Go faster!" The young man, out of spite, begins to run really fast – faster than he's ever run before on this track. Panting and stomping toward the old man, he finishes his run, saying, "You happy now, old man?" The old man smiles and says, "I'm happy today! We'll see how I feel tomorrow when you start running." Sometimes, our mentors will offend us for our benefit. Sometimes, their words will be a warm bath of kindness. No matter what, the words are always given in the spirit of service.

Giving

In the World's Greatest Student Leadership Team, one of the ultimate goals of the group is to provide everyone with at least ten seconds in the spotlight. The realization for many student leaders as they begin to adopt the World's Greatest message is, "No, you are not going to be the focus of the rally. In fact, you're not going to be performing in the rally!" In many cases, schools have student leaders who put on the rally, and the event ends up being more about them instead of others. Currently, you may get much fulfillment from being the person on stage receiving the acknowledgement for being in charge or for throwing such a great school event.

However, when you start to become fulfilled seeing other people in the spotlight, further gaining a sense of accomplishment for putting someone else as the focus, as the beneficiary of your efforts, even when that means that the other person is more appreciated and seen than you, the joy becomes seeing others receive the acknowledgement. You get a greater sense of fulfillment – greater than you probably ever have before – seeing another person whom you helped lift up take the stage and participate in a moment that he or she will remember for the rest of his or her life. It's not that you did the work for that person. It's not that you made up things about which to celebrate that person. Instead, you recognized a person's gifts and talents and then provided that person with a chance to be the focus of celebration, mentorship, and growth opportunities – moments to further become who he or she really is meant to become. Ultimately, you get the greatest sense of accomplishment watching others experience a significant moment because of who they are – because you made that moment possible. If you have the power to create a significant moment, that sense of fulfillment and achievement that another human being will feel, the ultimate reward is seeing another human being made better because you made it possible.

In many schools, the purpose of the leadership team is to celebrate and serve the Royal Family. You have to, as an individual student leader and as a whole student leadership team, ask, "Why do we do what we do?" If you aspire to be the type of school that helps each and every person become his or her World's Greatest Me, you have to be willing and able to place yourself outside the focus of attention. Often, your work must be stepping into the shadows so other people can enjoy the focused light of the celebration, rally, event, function, program, etc. Otherwise, what is your leadership team doing? Putting on the prom? Putting on the homecoming? Step back and ask yourself, "Why do we create prom?" and "Why do we create homecoming?" The purpose of your leadership class, if you are wanting to assist others in becoming their personal best, is to create significant moments for others, making sure that you include the Kileys, Alyssas, Austins, and Camo Kids in your focus. You have to decide: What is the purpose of your student leadership team? You have to give.

The Cycle of World's Greatest Mentors

So, first, you receive the mentorship of others. Second, you grow as a human being because of that mentorship. Third, because you are stronger and growing even stronger, you are able to be a mentor to others. Finally, these others grow and are able to become mentors themselves. The ultimate focus of your own leadership and your student leadership class is upon others. It's where you can say, "I understand my role. I'm going to feel good about watching others be celebrated. I'm going to feel a huge sense of privilege and gratitude by stepping back and seeing others lifted up. I'm not going to get the best by standing up on the stage and saying, 'Look at what I did.' It's that I get to say, 'Look at what I did for that person' and 'Look at how much they have benefited because I helped them.'" Imagine, for a crazy second, that you were a parent of a young girl. When your imaginary daughter took her first steps, said her first words, or rode a bike for the first time, you would not say, "Hey, KID! It's my turn for some attention! Stop hogging all the attention! It's my turn to look impressive!" You get the ultimate pride watching those under your care advance and become better human beings. You get great satisfaction knowing that you played a part in someone else's achievements. You get to be the proud mentor watching someone have his or her "diving board moment" where he or she gets to say, "Look at me!" **Your job as student leaders is to build the stage for others**, not yourselves. While most student leadership teams build a stage for themselves, you will build one for others.

How to Become Your World's Greatest Me

It's time to grow. It's time to step up, because others need you to step up. They need your care, your attention, and your mentorship. They need you to craft significant moments for them so they can be their best. You need others to do the same for you. The students around you need you more than ever. Here are four parting notes to get you started.

Uncovering

You have to be open and honest about who you are. You have to openly have the conversation with yourself about what you do well and where you fall short. In other words, develop a realistic understanding about what your gifts are. It's like the day that pictures from your school dance are distributed – watching fellow students, especially the girls, open the photo package, turn their heads to the side, and throw their noses up in the air, saying, "Oh, it's terrible!" Other people, naturally, come around and say, "Let us see! Oh, you look fantastic! What are you talking about? You look AMAZING!" You have to develop great picture-sense, knowing when you had a great moment and when you had one needing improvement, being able to evaluate truly who you are and how you are doing. From there, you can understand who you are today and where it's possible for you to be better tomorrow.

Simultaneously, we sometimes don't know what we are capable of doing until we are placed in situations that test us. It's like the football player who was told by his coach to run and run and run. The team was running forty-yard dashes, and the coach kept saying, "Okay, we're going to do another one!" The whole team began to moan in pain at the idea of doing another. Over time, this football player began to think to himself, "My goodness, I don't know if I'm going to be able to take another step!" He did not know if he could do it, but he quickly found out that he could push himself and take another step at that point where he did not even think that he could lift his foot at all. This football player, because of this challenging situation, learned something about himself. So, you have to put yourself in situations to be able to explore how great you can become. How many people are not given that opportunity to step up? How many students are rarely given the opportunity to do their best in what they are best at? How are they going to be able to explore that? You must mentor others in their strengths by creating the moments in which they can explore their abilities.

Developing Comfort in Your Own Skin

Chances are, you know someone who is not being him- or herself. You have to be comfortable enough in your own skin to be yourself. It's like the student who loved his huge metal belt buckle. It was a huge expression of who he was: flashy, showy, and ready for a party. However, on the first day of school, he was ridiculed for that belt buckle, and away it went into his drawer for the rest of high school until his senior year. Finally, on the first day of senior year, he felt confident enough to put on that belt buckle, shine it up, and walk around campus proud. You could see him walking from a hallway away. Security wondered if that belt buckle was a safety hazard. Birds were blinded by the reflection of light off this thing. Long story short, he loved wearing that belt so much that day that he wondered why he had not worn it the rest of his high school career. The challenge ahead of you is to show off that belt buckle from this point forward, even when it's scary to do so, because you know that this belt buckle was made for you.

What if the next few years went by and you became the most accepted and popular person at the school – but it was because you were faking who you were the entire time? Would that be worth it to you? As you start this journey, you have a chance to experience that it would be best to be the best you rather than you being the best version of someone else. What holds most students back from behaving in this way is insecurity and the threats that they perceive exist around them. Having worked with tens of thousands of students over the years, we can tell you firsthand that after high school, you'll rarely see 95% of these people whom you see each day (if not even less). This is your chance to be the best you, if you dare.

First-Step Mentality

Imagine, for a moment, what it was like to be a baby. When you took your first steps, what was the reaction of the people around you? When you fell down for the first time, what was that like? What did people say? If you can imagine this, you most likely cannot imagine a scenario where you stood up with shaky legs for the first time, took a step, and fell down, only to hear people screaming, "OH!!! BOOOOO!!! Horrible walking, kid. Just stay down! Don't try *that* again!" Frankly, if you saw someone saying such a thing to his or her baby, you probably would think about reporting child abuse. When babies are trying things for the first time, we applaud their attempts. We applaud them whether they succeed or they fall down – because falling down is simply part of the process of succeeding. However, when we get older, that way of seeing moments like these seems to change. Now, if someone tries something new around you at school, is that person applauded for the attempt? Is that person mocked when he or she fails? What would happen if you stood up on the top of your desk right now and announced that you were going to try out a new dance that you saw online today? Would your attempt be well received?

Becoming better and better at something requires that you take steps toward mastery. Many of those steps will end with you falling down – but it's the attempt to gain the experience that will help you become your personal best. Imagine what it would be like for others to respect your attempts at learning. What if students learned to walk for the first time when they were fifteen years old? What would that look like during lunchtime at school each day? As students who were newly learning to walk began to stand for the first time and took their first step, would their attempt be mocked? Chances are, instead, people would cheer – they would celebrate the failure as a sign that these new walkers were developing and improving. The first step on that particular day was their personal best. Simultaneously, the next attempt may exceed their personal best from before. One simple step leads to the next and to the next. Constantly, these students could take another step beyond what they had previously achieved. Why, then, can't everyone think this way about any form of learning? We're not quite sure how to answer, but you have a chance to take a "first-step mentality" about attempting to grow and failing. You can help other people by creating the opportunities for these first steps to occur.

Create Significant Moments

The most powerful thing you can create for anyone on your campus is a significant moment. That's your job as a student leader: to create significant moments for everyone on your campus. How will you acknowledge the

Kileys and Alyssas? The Austins? The Camo Kids? The Royal Family? It's not that this will show that you are in charge. In fact, many people might not even recognize that you did such an amazing thing for them. Creating a significant moment has no guarantee that it will be well received. However, it's the path for you to become your personal best: receiving the mentorship and assistance of others, helping others by creating significant moments for them, watching them take the stage and grow, and building up others to become the mentors of tomorrow. So, what is the purpose of your leadership class? Will you agree that it's to create significant moments? To mentor and build up others? To allow you to grow too?

BLUEPRINT QUESTIONS:

----

1. In your life, what significant moments have contributed to make you who you are?

2. What did the first five minutes of your most recent class communicate to you? What could have been done in the opening moments to communicate that you are wanted and needed?

3. To what degree do you think you can overcome the unique challenges in your life? Which challenges can only be overcome with the help of others?

4. In the past, in what ways has your student leadership team created a spotlight for

themselves? Who did not enjoy the spotlight during these moments?

DARES:

----

1. As a student leadership team, select one person or group on campus. Manufacture and carry out a significant moment that will communicate welcome, hope, and appreciation, where the spotlight is solely on others outside your team.

2. With a partner, share some challenges that you will need help to overcome. Identify a challenge, if possible, that you can help your partner meet and conquer.

THE VALUES OF

THE WORLD'S GREATEST HIGH SCHOOL

"THE WORLD'S GREATEST VALUES"

we are WHAT WE — BELIEVE

WHAT WE BELIEVE UNIFIES US •

NO ONE GETS Anywhere WITHOUT A TEACHER

ALL KIDS HAVE Futures

ALL STUDENTS ARE GIFTED & TALENTED

EVERY DAY IS AN OPPORTUNITY TO BECOME

THE WORLD'S Greatest ME

Everything WE DO WE DO WITH PRIDE

The World's Greatest Values.

CHAPTER FIVE

WE ARE WHAT WE BELIEVE

"What beliefs are being screamed from your hallways, restrooms, parking lots, classrooms, lunch lines, assistant principal offices, and on the potentially gum-filled underside of every desk in your school?"

As Chris, his doctors, his family, and his friends prepared for him to leave for Texas to receive extensive rehabilitation, everyone was of the same mind. Everyone believed that Chris had a future ahead of him and that each of their roles was to assist Chris in moving forward. Can you imagine, for a second, what it would have been like if one of his team of doctors did not believe that? What if one of the doctors believed that saving Chris, providing him with a chance to live a great life going forward, was not possible? How would that have impacted Chris? Would he be alive today if such a doctor was on that team? What if one of his family members had lost complete hope and would not speak to Chris during this time of healing and preparation? How would that have impacted Chris? Everyone on Chris's team believed the same thing: They believed that better days were ahead and that their job was to help Chris explore those future days in any way that they could. Like the beliefs of Chris's team impacted him, the beliefs of your team will have a profound impact upon your ability to make a difference in your school. The beliefs of your team may be the fundamental moment in your life that decides if you will make a difference in this school. Your team's beliefs could mean the difference between being available and able to help when a critical life-saving moment is needed. You could be met with a student who, quite literally, won't survive without your investment of time, emotion, and resources. The beliefs of your team could get in the way of you saving a life. What we believe matters.

In a critical moment, will you and your team take the right action? In a critical moment, what would be the cost of your inaction or lack of taking action? When Chris was injured and needed life support, what would have been the cost to Chris and everyone who knew him if they simply decided that it was not worth their time to save him? What if they did not believe that saving him was possible when it clearly was? They could have pulled the plug on him in this life-altering, life-saving moment simply by not acting at all. Quite similarly, babies are born daily who have arrived too early, who cannot breathe on their own, and who cannot survive without the help of others. No one looks at these young babies and says, "Hey! You down there! If you are not able to keep up, behave like a normal baby, be strong, and save yourself, we are not going to lift a finger to help you!" The thought of that is sickening. *How are you pulling the plug on your fellow students because of your beliefs and lack of quality action?* How is your anger, negativity, fear, and laziness hurting others? How is your inaction harming others? Your beliefs are where your actions are born. Your beliefs deserve your attention.

Right now, in the semi-comfort of wherever you are sitting, think about the greatest amusement park on the planet. Picture it in your mind. What is this place? What sights, sounds, smells, feelings, and tastes exist in this place? Think about all the things you can say about this place right now. Once you have done that, think about the people who work there. What do they look like? What do their name tags look like? Think about how these people act with their guests. Think about the general feeling produced by the actions of this place and the people within it. If you were to think of this place in detail, could you guess what these people believe? If there is another human being near you right now reading this book, ask that person what he or she thinks such a place as this believes, based upon how the people of this place act. Our guess about what you may say is this: When you are thinking about this place, chances are this place believes that relationships are very important. This place believes that relationships are the most important thing here. Truly, take a moment and write down all the things that this place probably believes about what it does and for whom it does it.

Now, picture your school. What is this place? What sights, sounds, smells, feelings, and tastes exist in this place? Think about all the things you can say about this place right now. Once you have done that, think about the people who work there inside and outside your leadership class. What do they look like? Do you know their names? Think about how these people act with their guests. Think about the general feeling produced by the actions of this place and the people within it. If you were to think of this place in detail, could you guess what these people believe? If you are like most leadership classes, it may be quite hard to talk at all about what this place believes. It can often feel like you know more about that amusement park, some distance away, than you do about your own school. The actions of those amusement park employees, which you experienced only a handful of times or less, feel more clear and meaningful than the actions you may have experienced by those around you who run your school. How can this be so? Turn back to that person with whom you spoke before, if such a person is nearby, and talk about what you think this school believes. If you cannot come up with much, think about how your school behaves. What do the actions of the people at your school say about what your school believes? The actions of those at your school communicate what your school believes.

Think back to that amusement park for a moment. The beliefs of this place and the people within it are on display everywhere. From the freeway exit, to the parking lot gates, the parking lot itself, the walkway to the front entrance, the ticket counters, the entrance, the streets within, to the sights within and beyond – everything about this place pours forth information about what it believes as a place and as a community of people. The people there don't simply talk about their lofty beliefs about why people matter; they behave like they mean it. Even if a person did not speak the language of anyone at this amusement park, this person would still leave (no words involved) knowing what this place believes and what to expect from this place in the future. The clear, unwavering actions of this amazing place are a model for the world about what it believes and how it lives out those beliefs daily in its actions – because actions speak louder than words.

What beliefs are being screamed from your hallways, restrooms, parking lots, classrooms, lunch lines, assistant principal offices, and on the potentially gum-filled underside of every desk in your school? Do these actions match up with what your school (or even your leadership team) is preaching out there on its posters or in its words? If you went through each and every hallway, classroom, gym, field, and office today and catalogued what all the posters, papers, and brochures said about your school, how many of these slogans, mission statements, values, or stated expected outcomes would you say that your school truly believes, as shown by its unwavering, regular actions? If you are like most schools, the answer is: few. What, then, does your school truly believe?

If you don't have a system of beliefs clearly on display through the actions of those on your campus, then what does your campus really believe anyway? Think about it: What do the actions of those walking your halls, sitting in your classrooms and offices, and playing and performing in your practice spaces say about the belief system of your school? Do these actions illustrate your school's belief that everyone matters? Do these actions show that your school is working to develop the individual greatness of each and every person on campus? Do they present that your school is willing to go to extraordinary lengths to make sure that each and every person gets a moment in the spotlight? Do these actions show that your school is built for everyone? If not, then who is your school built for? If not, then who is your school allowing to succeed while allowing others to fail? If not, who really matters at this school? If not, who gets the attention? Most important: How are you contributing to this as a leadership class?

What about your leadership class? What are the beliefs of your leadership class? What's the purpose of this place? If people did not know about your belief system, what would they guess about your beliefs based upon your actions as a team? What do your posters say about your beliefs? What do the events that you hold say about your beliefs? What does the power structure of your team and the way that decisions are made say about your belief system? So many leadership students look outside their classroom door and say to themselves, "If these people out here simply changed, simply wanted to participate more and have greater school spirt, THEN I could make a difference!" Instead, we want you to look at yourself and others on your student leadership team and ask, "What is the belief system alive in this room?" What is it?

Imagine a sports team where twenty-five team members were playing a different game. What kind of possibility of success would such a group have? Similarly, has your class defined the game that you are playing? Have you defined the belief system that will guide the actions of each of you inside and outside this room? Consider how most leadership teams operate. Older kids are living out the traditions of the school, almost blindly following the routine of what has been done year after year forever. If you ask such an older leadership student, "Why are we doing things like this?" he or she will probably answer, "Because we've always done things like this." These older students are often stuck in a pattern of celebrating the same kids in the same ways over and over again. It's not that they don't want to make a difference – it's that they are only making a difference for a small group of people. Their actions scream, "Not everyone matters." The younger students are often more open to change. They want to make things better, but they don't know exactly how to do that. Instead, they look to the older students for mentorship, guidance, and growth. They often say to themselves, "I don't know exactly what I'm doing, so I'm going to let one of the older students 'in charge' tell me what I should be doing." Sadly, the mentorship, advice, and advancement rarely come. Their actions say, "I don't feel like I have a say here until someone tells me I do."

This sloppy game plays out in the leadership team and every other place that such a team operates. Team members become event planners instead of changing lives and impacting futures or helping others explore their greatness. It brings mediocrity and hopelessness to a school, because the student leaders, those who can make the biggest difference, are not united in their beliefs – and their actions preach the message that not everyone matters at this school. Leadership teams with undefined beliefs and poorly intentioned actions only make more suffering around them. Your leadership team could be doing more harm than good!

Right now, your student leadership team could be caught in a tug of war. Naturally, the purpose of a tug of war is that both sides want to win. In a tug of war, there is a winner and a loser. It's possible that there is a tug of war of beliefs within your class. Some of your team members may believe that the purpose of this group is to recognize the unrecognized, while others may believe that the purpose of this group is to throw prom and homecoming. One group may believe that the purpose of this team is to create moments of significance for each and every person on campus, while another believes that the purpose of this class is to raise school spirit and put up posters. Until you and your team resolve this tug of war of beliefs, there will always be winners and losers inside your class. Frankly, as long as there is this tug of war going on in your leadership team, there will be far more people losing on your campus – the exact people whom you are supposed to be helping, you are harming through this conflict. The ultimate point that we are making here regarding beliefs and your leadership team is simple: You must all be pulling on the same side of the rope. You're all pulling on the same side of the rope to save students who are dangling off a cliff. You must all decide what you believe as a team. Until you do that, your team is operating in at least twenty-five different directions. Until you agree, your own commitment to greatness can only be *what you think you should be doing* instead of what the group agrees upon. You need to unify your beliefs.

Without unified beliefs, you may see some symptoms of dysfunction arising within your leadership team. You may see cliques forming, where one small group has all the power, while others are battling it out for whatever is left. Groups of students sit with one another day after day without interacting much with the other groups. Really, it may seem like your leadership class is more like six different leadership classes all meeting in the same classroom with the same teacher. The teacher may behave differently toward each of these groups depending on many factors, including how he or she feels about the group. One group may get lots and lots done, while others do not, barely getting anything done at all. Worse, in the absence of placing the emphasis on others, on the people whom a student leader is supposed to serve, student leaders in such a dysfunctional team create a spotlight of greatness that tends to focus solely on themselves.

If you do not teach the beliefs of your school or the beliefs of your leadership class, they will be taught anyway – even if the only voice doing the teaching is people's actions. The students at one school, for example, believed that they attended "Ghetto Valley High School." This became such a common way of addressing the school that when some state officials visited the school, students repeatedly welcomed them to "Ghetto Valley" and told them in many meetings that this was the most "ghetto" school they could attend. What were the beliefs at this school that made this a reality for these students? Were they wrong? If one student at your school had an idea about what your school believes, would he or she be right? What if four dozen had the same idea? What about then? How about if a few hundred had the same idea? If you don't take the time to discover the beliefs of your school and teach those beliefs, others will do the teaching for you – and you probably won't like what they are saying. Now, at this same school ("Ghetto Valley"), the student leaders teach the school's beliefs on the first day. Accordingly, there has been a huge change in how students regard the school – not because there are posters on the wall that claim this is the best school but because people teach that it is and behave according to those beliefs.

You must develop common language as a leadership class and as a school. If you have twenty-five different beliefs about the purpose of your leadership team, then you do not have common language. Your beliefs will define "who we are," "what we do," and "how we operate." If those are not clearly defined, then who are you anyway? What do you do? How do you operate as a class? It's time to agree upon some defined beliefs so you can answer these questions and act accordingly.

Consider: If you were to walk into a lunch area and sit down with random students and ask them to talk to you about what your leadership team is like, what would they say? Would they say...

"They really don't understand us,"

"They don't care,"

"They care only about themselves," or

"They only care about the Royal Family"?

How did they come up with that perception? Are they wrong? Keeping in mind that there's probably some evidence that informed their opinion about your team, how wrong are they *really*? Chances are, they formed these perceptions based upon the actions and behaviors they observed from your team. Your actions as a leadership team communicate who you are, what you do, and how you operate. When you have a lack of purpose, direction, and goals, chaos, suffering, mediocrity, and hopelessness often follow. Sadly, most leadership teams simply have never defined their beliefs as you are about to.

Why do we need these clearly defined? So you know why you exist in this leadership team and why the person next to you exists too. Beyond the classroom, all students, teachers, staff, parents, and beyond too should know who they are, what they do, and how they operate. If you are going to be the World's Greatest High School, you have to believe that you are going to be your personal best, your World's Greatest Me, so that those around you can be the World's Greatest *them*. Do you think you have World's Greatest Teachers? Students? Custodians? Parents? If not, then you are at Mediocre

High or No Hope High School. If you're at the World's Greatest High School, you and those you serve will know it, because you know who you are, what you are doing, and how you are operating – you are there to create significant moments and place a spotlight on each and every single person. Do you believe that your fellow students outside your classroom won't follow you? Don't care? Won't care? Then you are at Mediocre High or No Hope High School.

If someone walked into a faculty meeting at your school and said, "Tell me about your student leaders," what would they say? Would they say that you connect with and help engage students in the community? Would they say that you are an infringement on instructional minutes? Would they say that you only celebrate the popular kids? Would they say that you're "closed off" to outsiders and are filled with cliques? If they said any of these things, would they *really* be wrong? What evidence made them believe these things? How have you connected with and engaged each and every student on your campus? How have you regularly communicated that you are creating a community of hope around you? How have you supported and built kids' futures?

In short, it's time to define. It's time for you, your leadership team, and your school to define who you are, what you do, and how you operate. Until you define these, it's a mediocre or no-hope situation. It's not possible to be a world-class athlete without knowing that you are training to be world class. It's not possible for you to continually acknowledge every student unless you know that is your mission. You must start with your true essence – six words or fewer that communicate what you believe your purpose is and three bullet points about how you will go about living out your purpose. You are what you believe, and what you believe unifies you. It's time to unite and decide what you believe.

Define Your Purpose

Consider why you are sitting in this room. Why have you and your leadership team come together as a group? Look at the cover of this book that you are holding right now. Why in the world are you reading this thing? If your purpose as a student leader, leadership class, and school is to "help others explore greatness," then that could be your purpose. From there, you could consider how you would go about doing that. In three bullet points you could say that you (1) recognize greatness in others; (2) celebrate gifts, talents, and skills; and (3) spotlight greatness in any occasion. The idea here is simple but profound: name your purpose and list three ways that you will go about doing that.

At the beginning of the World's Greatest High School, when the first leadership team at this school was created, their purpose was "to put everyone in the spotlight for at least ten seconds." By defining this purpose, this allowed them to think about how well they were living this out as student leaders. After an event, the questions were, "How did we meet our purpose? Did we put everyone in the spotlight, or did we focus only on one sports team or group of teams? Did we provide each and every single student with the chance to feel significant, like they matter, and like they were expected to be present? Where did we demonstrate that everyone matters?"

If you walk into Mediocre High or No Hope High School and ask the student leaders, "Why do you only support and celebrate athletic greatness?" they will often reply, "Because we've been doing that forever! It's a tradition!" As a World's Greatest Student Leader, you know that this answer shows one thing they are missing: No one has sat down to define the purpose of the school, of the leadership team, or of being a student. "Purpose" is the heartbeat of your organization. If you don't have a heartbeat, then what is driving you, your team, and your school?

If you walk in and ask, "Why do we only support athletic greatness? It's the only thing we do," that can tell you that no one has sat down to define purpose. The essence of the purpose is your heartbeat – it's the heartbeat of your organization. If you don't have a heartbeat, then what is driving your team or school? So, creating your purpose is not as easy as simply "deciding." You have to tap into what makes you, your student leadership team, and your school tick. When you work with others to discover this heartbeat, the results can be pretty amazing.

At one World's Greatest High School, the purpose looked like this:

Gold and Blue Starts with Y.O.U.
Your personal best every day!
Own your future!
Understand we are one!

The student leaders and students pulled from every class on campus took five hours to put this together. It was not about what the student leaders thought was best. It definitely was not just about what the leadership teacher thought was right. Instead, everyone was represented when they tapped into this heartbeat. This purpose was not created out of thin air; it was found inside of themselves. It was found inside of the students who walked the halls of campus each day.

Another World's Greatest High School discovered their purpose to be...

Be your personal B.E.S.T. every day.
Be better today than yesterday.
Every day be my World's Greatest Me.
Support one another's strengths.
The future is in my hands.

Teachers, parents, staff, and students participated in finding this purpose and presenting it to the whole school, where each student committed to treat this as a daily promise.

Further, another World's Greatest High School located their purpose as follows:

O.W.N.ing your future starts with today.
Our actions and choices matter.
We are family.
No one gets anywhere alone.

The first day of school was dedicated to discussing this purpose and talking about what it would look like to live this out each and every single day.

As a leadership class, defining your purpose will have a significant impact upon how you will operate with one another. It provides the opportunity for you to say to a struggling or disruptive leadership student, "We notice that you agreed to this purpose, but are you really living that out as a student leader? You agreed to this! This is our belief system. You need to get on board, learn to get on board, or maybe it would be best to find another class or group." You cannot be in outright conflict to the purpose of your group. Disagreements are a natural part of working with a team, but being in conflict with the agreed-upon purpose of the group is not an option. Your purpose becomes the expectations of the class, because it defines who you are, what you do, and how you operate.

Once you define this purpose, it becomes one of the most important components of the class. The purpose was discovered, considered, and agreed upon. When you, your student leadership team, or your school does this for the first time, all will learn. Everyone will have taken part in putting this purpose on paper. However, in later years, what then? When you have new student leaders join you at the new semester, will they know about this purpose? Will they have the same level of agreement that everyone else had originally? Your purpose needs to be taught over and over again. When a new student arrives for the first time on your campus, that's the time when a student leader or two or three should teach this purpose. When the school year starts, that's the time when you need to teach this purpose to your new and youngest students. When a new student leader joins your team, it's time to teach.

Times will arise in your leadership class when you will find that some leadership students are not living up to the standard of this purpose. That's the time when you need to mentor these students. Times like these are when you have the opportunity to say, "You're not meeting the expectations. You're not growing! Can I help you?" It's your role to stretch the people around you to become their personal best. That's what you are expected to do every day for yourself: stretch. You are expected to help others do the same. However, at some point, you need to hold your purpose up and say, "Maybe this is not the place in which you can be your personal best." It's up to your team to make the decision of how much mentoring, time, and energy you give until it's time to help someone move to a better environment for him or her.

Your purpose becomes the grading system of the class. You, your peers, and your teacher can look to your purpose and say, "Where have I lived this out? This week, where did I give my best and grow as a result?" In a way, you are playing a game with, against, and for yourself. You get to play a game with others on your leadership team. You get to play an even larger game with your school as a whole. Are you living up to the purpose that you chose? One of the most powerful aspects of this is that YOU were the one to choose that purpose.

Think about how you will teach this purpose to your fellow students at your school. How could it be that students at your school know more about that amusement park that we mentioned at the start of the chapter than they do about their own school? How could it be that you could get a room full of thirty of your oldest students and say, "Tell me the purpose and beliefs of this place," only to find everyone in the room staring at you silently? How could it be that so many schools have little or no idea what their belief system is? It's because no one is teaching the purpose and the beliefs.

At one school, a group of ten student leaders sat with a representative of another World's Greatest High School who went to mentor this up-and-coming campus. The representative asked this student leadership group, "What is your purpose? What does your school believe?" There was absolute silence. Painfully, students kept looking at one another with that grave look of "Please someone, say something." The class president, who was not particularly participating in the activity, finally answered, "Well, I don't know what our purpose is, but I definitely believe that it's not possible for everyone to be important on this campus." Think about what it must be like to be a student leader working with such a class president. This guy was in leadership of the school for four years, and what he believed was that not everyone was important – and not everyone could be made to feel important. No one checked the purpose and beliefs of the school against what this fellow believed. How many people were harmed because no one was teaching the purpose and beliefs of the school? How many people felt like this was not the school for them because no one checked to see if this elected student official's purpose and belief system matched that of the student leadership class and school?

After you've discovered your purpose and beliefs, "first days" become quite important. What does the first day of school look like on your campus? Chances are, if you are like most schools, what you hear during this day sounds largely like, "Don't chew gum. Don't be late. Don't take your phone out." In those opening moments, the purpose and the beliefs of the school are communicated ("Don't, don't, don't"), whether you feel that accurately fits your school or not: This is what first days communicate. It's like meeting a person for the first time. Those first impressions matter. What would happen, instead, if you taught the purpose and beliefs of the school on purpose on these first days? How would that change your school?

What's wise to do campus-wide is also wise to do in your leadership class. Currently, how are the purpose and beliefs of your school and leadership class communicated during your first days between your fellow student leaders? How are the purpose and beliefs taught to new members of the class? What you begin here in this room, what you do with one another is the spark that will start a fire of possibility throughout your school. The way that you teach and mentor one another by defining your purpose and beliefs, holding one another to the commitment you each made to these, will have a profound impact upon who you are, what you do, and how you operate. From there, lives will change. Your school will change. Countless futures will be impacted because of what you do here. You have to teach and mentor your purpose and beliefs. You need to create a contract. Take the purpose and beliefs that you discovered and put them on paper. Add a line that says something like, "I agree to uphold and live out this purpose and values, inside and outside this classroom, working each day to become my personal best." Have each student leader sign, but ensure that you have a discussion about what it means to sign. If you sign this, you are committing to allowing others in this class to be part of your growth. If you sign this, you are saying, "Mentor me, even when that is not easy and may make me feel pressured, frustrated, angry, or uncomfortable." This contract is one way that you, as a student leadership team, can say, "These are our beliefs. We agree that this is what we believe." Define your purpose, create your six words or fewer and your three bullet points. Put them on paper. Discuss the importance of the contract. Have people sign.

Don't fall into the same trap that many schools have fallen into: This contract is typically created by teachers, administrators, and members of the Royal Family. Your school may be littered with posters proclaiming the mission statement of the school and the expected student learning outcomes. However, only a small handful of people years ago created these. No one is living them out – because few actually believe what these say. Schools such as these are not going to get past mediocre, because they have not defined the purpose of what they do. The rallies, celebrations, school spirit events, etc. don't match the stated mission or purpose of the school. Schools such as these say, "We have great traditions and great school spirit," but 30% of the students at the school won't graduate on time and may drop out. What, then, is the purpose of rallies, prom, and homecoming at such schools? To put the spotlight on those who have always had the spotlight – the Royal Family.

Everything you do comes back to the reason that you exist as a school, a team, and a student leader. Does your school exist for test scores? Does your school truly exist to build kids' futures. Your actions as a school will speak louder than words. When your actions say that your school is only for a small handful of people – because only a small handful of people are succeeding, receiving acknowledgement, and are given the resources to be healthy – then all those posters about you caring or you being a great school are simply artwork on the wall. As a team, come together to create and teach the culture. Have continual conversations about who you are, what you do, and how you operate.

Conversations About Greatness

When you look at your contract as a team or school, ask yourself what it looks like to be living that out each day. Who is doing what to accomplish this purpose? How are you and your team going to know if someone is truly living out this contract? The first year that you and your team create your purpose and define how you will go about achieving that purpose, it's easier for everyone to know and buy in, as long as these individuals were part of its creation. Everyone was part of creating your contract, so everyone had a say. However, in future years, this will not be the case. You will have to teach who you are, what you do, and how you operate to newcomers to both your student leadership team and your school as a whole. When new freshmen arrive, the freshmen of last year should step in and teach the new students about the culture of your school. When new members of your student leadership team transfer in at the semester, ongoing teaching of the culture between students should continue.

However, the conversations should continue on and on, regardless of whether someone joins your group or not. So what if you and your team created some contract four years ago? So what if the banner with your purpose has been hanging in the front of the school for the last year or so? You and your leadership team must have ongoing conversations about the greatness that you, your team, and your school community are seeing and experiencing. Further, you need to discuss your shortcomings as a team.

One student, named Polly, joined the student leadership team when she was a sophomore and her school was brand new. The students in the sophomore class were the oldest students at the school, over the freshman students. Each year for the next two years, the school would add another year of students until there were four grades of students walking through the halls. For the time being, however, Polly was one of the oldest students on campus. As the school was about to open its doors for the first time, Polly, the student leadership team, and much of the school community gathered to craft the purpose and goals of the school. Because of this work, traditions were taught from the first day. As new students would transfer into the school that first year, Polly would teach the culture of the school. New students were inducted into the culture of the school as Polly taught them this culture. This caught on with other students to the point that for that year and future years, they would teach the culture to incoming students and introduce them to the purpose and goals of the school. This pattern of students teaching students the culture of the school continues to this day.

When everyone has bought in and committed to the purpose and goals of your school, everyone is pulling the same end of the rope. At that point, the most pressing concern is to help others explore their greatness. Consider homecoming: Are you focusing only on the homecoming court or queen? How are you going to help others at homecoming explore their greatness? Consider everything and every event that you and your school does: How do you allow everyone to explore their greatness therein? You should be able to answer these questions through the purpose and goals that you created with your school.

Within your student leadership team, what about those who have not bought in or have not upheld your values? You should engage with such individuals in ongoing conversations about your purpose and goals. Over time, if problems still persist, you may have to ask, "Do we want to commit to helping these people be their best here in the student leadership team? Or is this the time when they need to move on to another place where they can be their greatest?" However, conversations that are of this "are they in or out" nature should be rare. Instead, you and your team should continue to talk about your unified purpose and goals. You should discuss where you fell short and where you met targets. You should ask yourself if you focused on the Camo Kids. Did you show that everyone matters? In situations where you only celebrated the football team, you should be able to see that as a violation of your culture if you say that "everyone matters." Have continual conversations about where your actions and your words align and where they don't.

As a team, take a look at The World's Greatest Values on the page after this chapter of this book. As you look at these, have conversations about if you are willing to consider adopting these as your own. Through the course of this book, we will be describing these values in more detail and how you can apply them in your life with your student leadership team. Further, we hope that your exploration of these values will lead you to consider where your actions and your words do not match. There will come a moment when someone is going to need you. There will be a time when a crucial moment will arise for a human being around you. Will you be ready to help that person? Will the beliefs that you hold allow you to provide the assistance that is needed? Talk about what you and your team believe before it's too late.

BLUEPRINT QUESTIONS:

----

1. Imagine the world's greatest amusement park. What does this place think is important? What does this place think about the people it serves? Give examples.

2. Now, consider your school: What does your school think is important? What does your school think about the people it serves? Give examples.

3. What is the purpose of your school's student leadership team? What do they do? How do they do that?

DARES:

----

1. As a student leadership team, gather a focus group of five student leaders, your leadership teacher, and fifteen to twenty students who are not from your leadership team. Don't select the usual volunteers! Ensure that you are including representation from your entire school, including the Kileys, Alyssas, Austins, and Camo Kids. Ask this focus group the Blueprint Questions above. Discuss. Write down what is said.

2. In teams of three, interview random students on campus asking the above Blueprint Questions.

Don't select the usual volunteers! Ensure that you are including representation from your entire school, including the Kileys, Alyssas, Austins, and Camo Kids. Consider video recording their responses.

3. As a student leadership team, gather a focus group similar to the one discussed above. With this group, define the purpose and beliefs of the entire school.

4. During an event that you are hosting, take one photo of people watching and being in the action of the event. Discuss the photo. Who is engaged? Who is not engaged? Who did you include? Who did you force to simply sit and watch?

CHAPTER SIX

ALL KIDS HAVE FUTURES

"It's your job to plug people in so they are more likely to make the future of their dreams a reality."

Chris's mom was an intensive care unit nurse. After Chris was safely in the care of doctors, she used her expertise to search for the best rehabilitation center in the country that could help her son. Because Chris was taking experimental medication, options were limited, but his mother was able to find a world-class rehabilitation center for injuries like those Chris suffered. The plane ride to Texas was exceedingly boring. The inside of the airplane, even though it was a medical aircraft, was as boring as the interior of any plane – the chief difference being that Chris was restrained and unable to move through the flight. After he arrived in the Lone Star State and was shuttled to his new home for the coming months, he met his new roommate. Caesar, an ex-gang member who was the target of an assassination attempt, had experienced a similar injury to his spine as Chris had. Caesar and his family were checked into the center under a false name so that the person who attempted to kill him would not come back and finish the job. As far as Chris and the staff were concerned, Caesar was like any other teenager who needed help. He and Chris developed a temporary friendship while they were there, often sitting outside seeing how far they could spit cherry pits across the lawn. Though Caesar had a criminal past, he was treated the same as every other young person there, including Chris, receiving rehabilitation assistance. This was one of the best places on earth to heal one's body after a spinal cord injury, and the staff acted as if all the patients there, regardless of their past, were deserving of the same level of care and investment. Regardless of Caesar's past, they were going to help him. Everyone acted as if Caesar could have a future ahead of him, one they could assist in building. Does your school operate with such faith in its students?

The fundamental belief of the World's Greatest High School Student Leader is that **all kids have futures**. Whether that future is as a brain surgeon or as a person locked up in a prison, each and every student on your campus has a future. Unlike the general practice of many people at your school – seeing students in terms of passing or failing, succeeding or failing, and graduating or not – student leaders at the World's Greatest High School see that every student is going somewhere. Take a look at the students around you right now in class. Where are they headed? Some of these people will live long, fruitful lives. Some will have lives shorter than they expect – yet happy ones nonetheless. Others may have long lives of pain. The possibilities are endless. When you think about each person on your leadership team, you can see how who he or she is today can greatly impact the quality of that future later on. However, thinking about the future of these fellow students in these terms is the rarity. Many people on your campus are quick to categorize your peers as successes or failures, as part of the Royal Family or not, as people who are "in" or people who are not. Many people at your school would be quick to judge your peers (and perhaps you) based upon what little they know about them. After all, at many schools, they provide awards for members of the Royal Family voted "most likely to succeed," "best sense of humor," "best smile," "most athletic," or "class clown." Many would be quick to say, "This student does not have a future." Many will give up on your fellow students. What gives them that right? What gives anyone the right to pull the plug on anyone? What gives you the right to simply let that happen?

Consider one of your worst or weakest moments in your life. Would it be appropriate or fair for anyone to judge you and your ability to live a good life based upon that single moment? Your appearance? Popularity? What about your performance on a single test? Should your entire future be determined by a single test in a single class? What about your grade in an entire class? Should your whole future be determined by the grade you received one year early in your middle school or high school career? Naturally, the answers to these questions are "no." However, is that not what we do to people each and every single day on our school campus? Have you based your opinion of someone upon a single first impression? Have you made judgements about another based upon his or her performance in one skill, one class, or one conversation? Have you "written off" or dismissed other people in your heart or mind because of your interaction with them one day? If you are human, you have! If you truly believe that all students have futures, as a student leader, you have a responsibility to see the potential in others and help them grow that potential so that they can live the best lives possible.

One skill or lack of skill does not make or break a future. Some students have math skills. Some students have language skills. Some students have writing skills. Others have music skills. Others have speaking skills. Even others have dancing skills and many, many others. However, if you were to judge a person's future based upon just one of these skills alone, many would seem to have a future ahead of them, while many others would not. At your school, students are judged by their abilities each day by their peers. It may seem as if the very worth of someone is determined by his or her ability to do well in one single skill. Further, many students are judged not just by their ability to perform a skill well but by their ability to not fail or be seen as trying to do better. How many times have you seen a student ridiculed for simply trying? If the future world's greatest basketball player was a freshman on your campus today, that person may feel ashamed to try to throw the ball out of fear of what other people thought. This person could be categorized as a failure if he or she obtained a D in his or her math class. If everyone judged everyone else based upon one skill *today*, some would have a future, while others would not. In the case of this basketball player, this would be quite short sighted: later on, he or she will be the best in the world. However, if people judge futures based upon one type of ability today, few people are winners. Few people are able to feel like they are part of something meaningful, because they are being told that they have no future. The World's Greatest High School Student Leader sees others in terms of what they can become tomorrow and in the future.

One student, for example, had poor writing skills. For years, she struggled with her writing and was getting extra help that would assist her in passing her classes, scoring well on college entrance exams, and excelling as she went into college and beyond. One day, when she went to go see her guidance counselor about her class schedule for the coming year, it was recommended to her that she not take classes that would help her get into college because she was "not the kind of person who went to college" because of her lack of writing skill. While it was true that she would need to improve, would need to greatly work on her writing, and may need to go to community college to prepare her for going on to a four-year university, did this guidance counselor have the right to say that this student should pull the plug on her college dream? At the World's Greatest High School, this counselor would have helped this student in any way that he or she could to get her one step better than the day before and would have seen her not in terms of her lack of skill but in terms of who she could become tomorrow and in the future. Likewise, it's up to you as a student leader to see the potential futures of those around you. As a student leader, you are not in the business of pulling the plug on the futures of others. It's not your job to make others feel like failures. *It's your job to plug people in so they are more likely to make the future of their dreams a reality.*

You can help people make or break their futures. The way that you interact with others around you will have a direct impact upon the future that they enjoy. No matter what, they will have a future, but you have the ability to make them more able or less able to have the ultimate future that is possible for them. That's how serious your job is as a student leader. You can harm the futures of others. You could behave in such a way that only alienates others. You could celebrate only a small handful of students on campus and make everyone else feel like they don't belong. That will have a huge impact upon their futures for sure! Further, you could ignore their futures and say, "Their futures are their business! We have our own problems to deal with!" You could leave them to figure things out on their own. Some of them will be fine. Many others will not do as well as they could have with your help. Alternatively, you could take as much responsibility for helping others build their futures as possible. You could see every interaction you have with any other student as a chance to help that student become his or her World's Greatest. You could make it your personal and team mission to help others explore their greatness and *actually* help them get closer and closer each day! You could make the purpose of your day to support and explore your greatness today, tomorrow, and beyond – and to help others be supported in the same way. People need you more than you know. There are students around you each day who will live or die because of what you do as a student leader – this is not an exaggeration. Will you alienate others, or will you invite them in? Will you exclude or will you include? Will you take responsibility, or will you leave others to fend for themselves? You get to decide, and the choice *is yours*. As a student leader, others are depending on you – even if they don't yet know it.

Leadership class is not about painting posters and putting on the prom; it's about building your future and the futures of others. Your job is to **change lives and impact futures**. Put simply, you have a choice in how much you help others become the future versions of themselves. If you help them, they will be better for it. If you help one another, how much stronger will you all be? By creating significant moments for others, you could change how they see themselves, how they interact with others, and how they relate to school. Without you, others will suffer. That's how important you are: You mean the world to people on your campus whom you have not yet even met. It's time to prepare to help these people. First, explore what you believe about "all kids have futures." Then, consider what you alone can do for others around you. Third, talk with your student leadership team about what you all believe about "all kids have futures." Finally, decide how your team will go about assisting others in this work.

Together, let's discuss how you can go about assisting others at your school as if all kids have futures.

What You Believe and Do Matters

First, as an individual student leader, you can develop your ability to understand and see the future possibilities for other students at your school. Potentially, there was a time when you walked onto campus thinking only of yourself: "What classes do I have? What grades can I obtain? What future can I get as a result of how well I do here?" While those questions may still hold great importance to you, you cannot call yourself a student of the World's Greatest High School if you are solely focused upon your own advancement and well-being. How much impact could you have upon others if you thought *you* were the only person worth your time during your day? There are specific ways of thinking about and acting within your world and with those in it that become of great importance when you are thinking about changing lives and impacting futures of the students around you each day. Here are a few to consider:

Everyone Is an Ace

What would it be like to regard every person as fundamentally worth your attention? As a student leader, it's far too easy to fall into the trap of only wanting to help those who are the easiest to help or those whom you perceive as deserving your assistance. For example, think about a student at your school who treated you poorly at some point in your past. Would this be a person whom you would consider assisting toward the future of his or her dreams? What about students who are not easy to communicate with? Think about those students who are not in the front rows of your celebrations and rallies cheering but are in the back silently sitting, looking down at their phones. It's not easy to think about how you could help individuals who don't seem to want to take part in the blessings that you have created for your school. As a student leader, the biggest temptation is to help those who are most like you, most in your reach, and most, in your judgment, worthy of your respect and attention. What happens when you drop that way of thinking – when you stop thinking of people as a "two," "five," or "seven" and regard every person as if he or she were a well-deserving ace? What's possible when you treat other people with heart, even when they may not have earned it?

At a recent twenty-year class reunion, Jason, a former student leader, was approached by an individual whom he did not recognize, who said, "Jason, you probably don't remember me, but I need to tell you something. Twenty years ago, I was a stranger walking down a hallway, and you came up to me and said something random about making 'today the best day of your life.' I just wanted to tell you that you did not know it at the time, but I was out of school in the hospital that previous week because I had attempted suicide. You walking up to me and talking to me, even when you did not know me, meant the world to me. Thank you." Where would this stranger be if Jason had not been at school that day and had not greeted this other student? No one can say for sure. However, Jason did not wait for an invitation to be a small part in making this other student's life better. Jason did not make judgements about this other student's worthiness to receive his help. Instead, Jason simply operated as if anyone whom he saw mattered. Like Jason, you could mean the world to someone today as long as you are willing to help without condition. Treat everyone as someone who needs you and deserves you. Your actions should convey that everyone matters.

Focus on Ability, Not Disability

Ask people to picture a student leader, and they often imagine some outgoing kid who has lots of energy, has big plans, and is able to talk to hundreds of students at the same time. However, if you look around your student leadership class, there are many types of students with different areas of expertise sitting around you. You probably have fairly quiet students who are experts at getting focused tasks completed. You have other students who are artistic. You have others who are great organizers. You have others who are great advertisers, able to speak to anyone, seemingly without fear. When you have a narrow definition of what success looks like, you'll find few successes. In your leadership class, you should see a microcosm of the school: many abilities – not the same abilities. You can look around at your teammates and say, "I accept your strengths and will help you develop more and more into your personal best." In your leadership class, you should focus upon the abilities of those in your student leader family. You can help them discover those abilities. You can help them grow in those abilities. Is this how the school operates as a whole?

Are "abilities" the focus of the day-to-day lives of students, teachers, administrators, and parents on your campus? If you are like many schools in the nation, the answer is "no." The majority of time may be spent focusing upon the disabilities or lack of abilities of students. You may have students on campus who will develop into leaders in their families and cities but don't have the self-control required quite yet. You may have students who are going to be some of the hardest workers at their places of employment or business, but they haven't yet mastered the ability to arrive on time. You have other students who will be healers and coaches who will help others reach their optimum body and spiritual health, yet they have not gained what's required to be awake before 9:00 in the morning. You may have others who will be amazing parents but don't have great home situations right now that allow them to dress as expected – or encourage them to dress as required by the school's rules. When you focus squarely upon instances where students are missing the mark, what kind of place does that make your school? While it's important to have rules and important to help students become better and better, is the focus upon the lack of ability (misbehavior, disability, or lack of academic success), or is it upon the potential strengths of your fellow students?

We want to hold people accountable to their ultimate potential, not constantly beat them with where they are failing. At the World's Greatest High School, one student was habitually absent. After a week away from class, the young man returned to class to be met by his student leadership teacher. At this point, the teacher could have said, "Tony, you are an absolute failure. You never show up to class. You're never going to graduate." Instead, because this teacher focused upon strengths, he welcomed the student back to class, saying, "Tony, you are our best operator of the sound equipment. When you are absent, we feel like part of our body has been cut off. We need you. Please come to class as much as you can, because we are not the same without you." Consider what this experience was like for this student. Instead of feeling like it may have been a good idea to miss another day of school, he felt as if missing any more would have had an impact upon him and his team. He felt like he belonged there. He felt like he belonged there because there was a relationship. That relationship was focused upon growing him in his abilities, not trashing him with his lack of ability. In your daily interactions with other human beings at your school, focus on ability. YOU, personally, may be the only reason someone wants to even show up.

Focus on Awe, Not Flow

Ideally, students come to class to learn. Learning involves failure. That's a natural part of learning: failing. Learning could be said to be a process of awe, where the point of learning is to find oneself in an unknown place, where one finds out more and more about this place, and where one finally has a transformational experience of some kind. It's like not knowing anything about the pyramids, seeing them for the first time, having the desire to learn about these amazing things, and, finally, knowing something about the Egyptians. Think about a time when you learned something that interested you. Chances are, you did not know much about that thing before the lesson or situation involving the learning began. What you were struck with, potentially, was a feeling of surprise, interest, shock, or, most poignantly, "awe." Awe is a feeling of wonder or interest. What would it feel like to enter any unknown subject or situation with this feeling? What would it be like to believe that any learning experience has the potential to make you better than the day before?

Go to most high school classrooms in the United States and you'll find that many students don't want to ask or answer questions out of fear of being seen negatively. Why is this? Isn't it natural to not know things, so that way one can learn? There is so much focus upon "not knowing" as a flaw, as a negative, that few people want to be in a position of not knowing. Few want to be in the "flawed" position of getting anything wrong. How far can one really get in life without being wrong? Can one learn to walk without making a mistake?

Can one learn to play an instrument or ride a bike without messing up? Can one learn to speak a foreign language without error? Can one write the perfect essay on the first day of high school? Will you be the perfect *you* today? The journey of learning is not about "not being flawed." The purpose of learning is to fail better and better, to experience the awe of learning, and to place yourself in a position to do your best – so that you can do your best even better tomorrow. We call that "learning."

In short, one of the most powerful ways in which you can assist others (and yourself) in having an optimal future is by seeing others through the glasses of "I see your gifts. I want to help you grow your gifts." It's time to do away with seeing others in terms of their flaws, their failures, and their social position at the school. Everyone deserves your assistance. Everyone is worth your time. Everyone has something to offer. Everyone has value. Everyone needs you. In the most basic sense, others simply need you to believe in them. Others need you to look at them with those eyes of belief that scream, "I can see you. I'm so happy you are here. I believe in you. I'm in this with you." You can't turn that into a poster and expect that to have the same impact as you actually believing these ways of thinking. Each day, make it a point to see others more and more with these eyes.

Say Hi

You have the power to change someone's life. You, personally. Just you. Sure, your whole leadership class could be involved in the process, but in the end, today, walking down the hallway, you could utterly and completely change the life of another individual. You could change someone's life for the better. It could be a moment of great importance to that person to simply have one other human being look him or her in the eye and say, "Hello." You could change that person's life for the worse – by simply being another face in the crowd who couldn't care less. For some, your eye contact, your "hello," your smile, anything, could be the one thing in their life that says, "I am important. I am worth it." As a student leader, your personal job is to enhance the well-being of each and every person you come into contact with during your day. Your job is to provide the elements of love and life in the lives of others around you. Your job is to give those whom you care about (hopefully everyone) that which is required for them to thrive. When someone experiences your acknowledging him or her, that will help define his or her world. When someone experiences your blessing him or her in a way, this will have a huge impact upon how that person does within the world of your school.

Candy was a Camo Kid at the World's Greatest High School who was placed in the student leadership class because she needed elective credits to graduate. Candy did not want to participate in anything. She would have never self-selected to be in a leadership class. So much of her school experience was spent blending into the crowd, being the silent kid in the class, being as much unseen as possible; she felt this was the safest strategy for her. Every single day, one of the student leaders in the class would say "hello" to Candy. Candy would barely reply, looking at this other student. This went on for three months until, one day, Candy started to say hello back. A few weeks later, she started to volunteer her opinion in class. A couple weeks after that, she was sharing almost more than the teacher could handle. Within a month, the teacher was having Candy lead small-group activities. By the end of the school year, Candy was running the rallies in front of 2,000 students. All of this started because one person, without fail, said "hello" every day. A welcoming word, simply noticing another person, is a powerful thing. From whom are you withholding your power?

Mentor Someone

Mentoring is the act of building up another person. It does not mean that you are the person's gym boot camp coach screaming at him or her to get fit, get studying, or show up to class on time. Mentoring is the act of recognizing a need and assisting another human being in meeting that need for his or her own well-being. Mentoring another could mean (as discussed above) saying "hello" to that person each day. It could mean that you are there to tear in half your morning muffin to give that person a bite to eat. It could mean that you are asking the person if you could call him or her if you run into any trouble with the homework (as a chance for you to talk to that person about his or her homework too). It could mean that you ask that person to be present with you at a big life event, like a fifteenth or sixteenth birthday party or otherwise. Any chance that you have to personally build up another person through your actions, that's part of your job as a student leader.

When Gary was fourteen, a junior leadership student invited him to his house because his computer was broken and he knew that Gary was great at fixing computers. He compensated Gary by paying him in junk food for a couple days. This junior leadership student could have called the local electronics store and paid loads of money to get his computer fixed – but instead, he took the opportunity to ask this short, thin, freshman kid into his house. He was not taking advantage of Gary's weakness; he was putting Gary in a position to use his computer skills as an advantage. Gary got great food and a friend out of the interaction. This was a significant moment for Gary. He was then invited to bring his gifts to the student leadership class and ended up being in charge of the technology in class. This is what mentoring is: helping another human being be better, happier – a better version of him- or herself.

Stretch Someone

You can also change the lives and impact the futures of others around you by stretching others and their abilities. There are students in your class who, potentially, will have mammoth skills in the future but have yet to fully develop these. One of your jobs as a student leader is to work with them in those abilities, to stretch them to their full potential, and to help them release those skills into the world. Without you, they can't work on those abilities or be stretched. Think about a rubber band laying on a desk somewhere at your school. Right now, without anyone involved, it's just a connected circle of rubber laying there. If you get involved with that rubber band, you could begin stretching it and stretching it until it's reached its ultimate possibility and power. You could, from there, release it to zoom into the world. Just as with that rubber band, you could do this with others around you. There are students in your leadership class and in your school who may become great men and women one day – but they can't do that without you. We often think about star athletes who were fortunate enough to have become involved in their sport. What if they did not sign up or never went to engage in that sport with friends? Would they have reached the ultimate level? Without coaches, mentors, and others involved in their growth that stretched them, would they be the world-class athletes that they are today? Athlete or not, everyone needs a mentor to stretch them. Could you be that kind of mentor for another?

What We Believe Matters

What your team believes matters. How your team regards the futures and possibilities for students around you matters. Think back to the purpose and the beliefs that you named in the previous chapters: How you operate a student leadership class will be greatly defined by how you regard students' futures and your ability to shape those futures.

Are They Worth It?

How many times do we bless others with an agenda?

Often, dysfunctional student leadership teams make statements such as, "We would do something for *those* students if they simply would show more spirit," or "We won't try that again, because only a few people showed up the last time," or "We did not get the appreciation we expected, so we're not going to put ourselves out there to be hurt." Statements such as these show the focus of these student leaders: themselves. The people who they feel are most "worth it" are themselves. The success or failure of an event or campaign is entirely defined by the ways that *they* are impacted by it. As a student leadership class, you cannot be the focus of the blessings. The student leadership class is not meant to be a place where you get to be in power to throw your own parties. This is "No Hope" or "Mediocre" (at best). Instead, you have to ask yourselves, and behave accordingly, "Do we believe that others are worth us giving up our position on stage, our place of power, or our own recognition or appreciation?" If the answer is "no," we strongly recommend that you disband your student leadership team and hire a new one. You have to believe, in your heart, that the whole purpose for your team existing is to change the lives and impact the futures of others – most specifically those unrecognized, unseen students on your campus. Your team exists to create Rose Petal Moments for everyone on campus.

Can We Survive Without Being Thanked?

As student leaders, your work will often feel lonely outside your team. While your team members will have one another, there will be many moments where you will feel that you were not fully appreciated for your hard work. Why does this feeling arise for most student leaders? Most often, student leaders fail to recognize what truly makes the mark of a "successful" celebration, rally, or campaign. The success is not a room full of screaming people. The success is not having the principal, teachers, and dozens of students gushing, "Thank you, thank you, thank you," as they hang a colorful banner above your door or buy you donuts (though those are all great things). The true mark of success is not you all receiving a thank you: Success is when you put someone in the spotlight who would not have had that opportunity without you. In your core, you get to know that you played an integral part in shaping the future of an individual – because there are no small moments on stage. As a student leader, you have to believe that the greatest joy is putting another human being in a position of recognition in place of yourself.

What About Failure?

As a student leadership team, know that failure is part of your journey. Unless you have failed in the past, there is simply no possibility for you to make something better today for the students whom you serve. If you are reading this in the hallways of No Hope High School and you recognize that things need to change, at least that is a beginning. When you and your team agree that you have failed others in the past, have placed yourselves in the spotlight when you should have placed others there, and have alienated some students into invisibility, this is a chance for you to make life for your fellow students and community better. Failure is the ultimate starting point for future success. It's up to you to do the hard work to rise up.

What We Do Matters

As we draw this chapter to a conclusion, here are a number of ways that you can change the lives and impact the futures of students on your campus as a team. As we discuss each, remember that it's up to you to make these things happen. There are no small leaders in the World's Greatest Student Leadership Team – everyone has the power to build up another human being or tear him or her down. Which will you do each day?

Orchestrate Mini-Experiences

Not everything you do has to be a rally. Not everything you do has to be on the same scale as prom, graduation, or the first day of school. In fact, much of what you will do as a student leadership team involves small, fifty-minute-or-less challenges. Think about what will tell another student that he or she is individually recognized and seen. This is where so many student leadership teams get it wrong. What makes the greatest impact on another human being is not being one of a few hundred being recognized; it's the personal touch, knowing that another human being specifically took time to acknowledge him or her. Instead of putting up on the wall the more than one hundred names of students who made the honor roll, printing out as many certificates that are clumsily delivered to classes, make it personal. Write a personal note to a student who you know has improved his or her skill in some way. Perhaps this student is sitting next to you in class right now. This note does not have to be long. It does not have to be poster-sized. A personal note on a small 3" x 5" index card is far more meaningful for an individual than simply being another name on the wall. What would happen if you made most of the activities of your student leadership class focused upon engaging in small-scale, personal, intimate interactions with students instead of blanketing campus with posters that are quite impersonal?

One student leadership team purchased two hundred apples and handed one to every student who walked through the front gates of the school, saying, "Give this to the person who inspires you most and tell them why." Later that day, when the student leadership students were in class, a teary-eyed math teacher walked through the door with a giant bag of apples. "This," he said, "has been the best day I've ever had as a teacher." That day, over twenty students came to his room and thanked him, telling him how he had helped them. This benefited both the students and this teacher. Do you think the futures of these students and this teacher were made better because of this? Even what you consider to be a small endeavor is of huge importance to those who are the recipients of your acknowledgement.

Defy Social Norms

As a student leader, you probably are already defying social norms. The norm may be to remain silent, to not "make a fuss," to not draw attention to oneself or another, to not say or do anything that makes one vulnerable. However, the lives and futures of those you serve depend upon you to bravely step out of what's comfortable and take risks on their behalf. You may need to walk up to someone you don't know and greet him or her. You may need to tell a teacher that he or she has changed your life. You may need to ask for help. You may need to challenge your administrator or teacher that things could be better and that you want to be part of making things great. You may need to sit with the principal and explain to him or her why less time should be spent on dress code and more time should be spent on making people feel welcomed, needed, and wanted. You will have to learn how to do all of this while maintaining the highest level of respect, professionalism, and bravery – because none of this will be easy.

Today, you and your student leadership class are changing your lives and futures. Now that you know that you have such power over the lives and futures of others, you have a huge choice in front of you: Do you risk everything, go "all in," and work each day as if you are the student leadership team that is, quite literally, going to "save the world" for your fellow students? Alternatively, are you going to make this class about prom and posters, celebrate the Royal Family, and further alienate and harm those around you? The choice *is* yours. You will make this choice in every single thought, conversation, and action you take alone and as a team. Choose to rise up to what you have been called to do: to *change lives and impact futures*. After all, if you were in Chris's position, would you not want those around you to acknowledge, bless, and gift their skills without measure? You have so much power to save the lives and futures of those around you. Will you help them?

BLUEPRINT QUESTIONS:

----

1. Personally, how much of your business is it if another student takes steps toward the future of his or her dreams? Do you care? Why?

2. In terms of the work of the student leadership team, what skills are you not particularly good at?

3. What are some ways others can help you when these skills are needed?

4. How is failing at a task or challenge treated at your home? In your student leadership class? In other classes? What are some ways in which your fellow student leaders or leadership teacher have made you want to avoid failing or avoid participating?

DARES:

----

1. On your own, live one hour of today as if everyone and everything was worthy and deserving of your attention and care. Pay strong attention to people and events during this hour.

Record your experience in a one-page journal response.

2. On your own, select a student leader in your class with whom you don't normally speak. For one week, observe this fellow student leader. Notice what unique abilities he or she has and how he or she contributes to the health and well-being of the class and team. Write down what you see. At the end of the week, walk up to that person and read what you observed to him or her. (Instructor note: Consider purposefully pairing students for this activity.)

3. Say "hello" to three people you don't know every day this week.

CHAPTER SEVEN

NO ONE GETS ANYWHERE
WITHOUT A TEACHER

"Imagine yourself standing at the back of high school graduation, knowing that each and every student sitting in the seats around you was impacted in some way because of your involvement with student leadership."

While in Texas, Chris had many teachers in the form of rehabilitation specialists who were assigned to strongly encourage him to stretch and rebuild his abilities while giving him the chance to learn about what best he could give in his body movement. During these initial periods of rehabilitation, he would sit in his wheelchair in his room and attempt to move himself down the hallway to his appointment. It would often take him forty-five minutes to move only fifty feet down the hall. Some of his teachers there believed in him. They provided him with the chance to test the limits of his abilities. Others were not such great teachers, as they would tell Chris, without much evidence, that he would be unable to do certain exercises because of his injury. In the eyes of some, he was failing from the start. He had some relationships that were encouraging. He had others that were challenging. One specialist, for example, would not believe Chris that he could feel his legs fighting to speed up or slow down the exercise bike. At some point in Chris's recovery, he started to feel like he might be able to move his legs slightly. During the cycling exercise, he could intentionally slow down and stop the cycle from automatically moving by concentrating on this legs. When he told the specialist, she was in complete doubt: "Chris, that's not possible with your injury." Chris, quite indignantly, protested, "Tell me when to slow down the bike, and I'll slow it down! Tell me when to stop it!" He could easily follow through on both challenges. Still, some did not believe that it was possible that he was capable of doing it. Others, though not entirely sure of the possibility of Chris having any movement in his legs, allowed Chris to explore this ability. As some doubted him, he said, "Whatever you tell me I can't do, I'm going to fight to do it." As others praised him on, he used that liberty to stretch and learn. Like you, Chris had great teachers, and Chris had some teachers who were not exactly who he needed them to be. These relationships had great power over his ability to challenge himself and grow. Some relationships build you up. Some tear you down.

You can't fully help another person without a relationship. While you can give away money or items to an individual, you can give him or her clothing to wear, and you can give him or her food to eat, how much can you truly improve that person's life without building a relationship? When you engage in gift giving, you can provide for the health and safety of another human being. You could even provide for a greater well-being in life overall. However, if you want to provide a sense of belonging, if you want to help another person live optimally within your school community, or, perhaps, if you want to provide another human being with the opportunity to become the ultimate version of him- or herself, a relationship with that person is a basic requirement; otherwise, you're just throwing gifts his or her way. Potentially, you are engaged in acts of giving today. You are putting up posters. You are writing cards. You're wrapping up candies or other goodies and sending them to students, teachers, staff members, etc. However, it feels like there is something missing. People are not responding as you wish. People are not advancing as you had hoped. You're feeling this because a relationship has not been fully fostered. Central to your work as a student leader are relationships.

How many "friends" or connections do you have on social media? If you are anything like the authors of this book, you have hundreds, if not thousands. Are these people really your friends? Depends how you define "friend." The type of relationship that you must build with others around you on your campus cannot be simply that of *friend* in the sense that most people use this word. Instead, you are to be a special type of friend: one who mentors, one who teaches. You can become a teacher – one who mentors others to assist them in growing. You can also be the connector who assists other teachers in building relationships with students. Rather than clumsily befriending every person you see without any real care or regard for these individuals and their needs, an intimate connection with each person you wish to help is yours to foster. As a teacher, even if you are fourteen years old, you can help build up another person. You can have a special relationship with others around you.

Why can I remember the names of some teachers and not others? Why is it that a person can remember the name and face of his or her first-grade teacher, being able to recount specific instances and events within class with exceptional detail, but be completely unable to even recall the name of his or her third-grade teacher? How is it that you may even be able to remember the name of your kindergarten teacher, when you were only four or five years old, but you cannot remember the name of a teacher you had only a few years ago? Chances are, thinking back on these teachers whom you can actually name, they had a profound impact upon you. Potentially, they may have harmed you; they may have been nightmares of human beings. Alternatively, they may have had a special relationship with you: one where they grew you as a human being, making you better each and every single day because of who they were and what they did in their classroom. Other teachers, ones whom you don't even remember, may have delivered all the required lessons but failed to be anything but another acquaintance in your life. Which type of teacher will you want to be as a student leader?

If you want to be the type of teacher, mentor, or leader who greatly impacts the lives of others around you, you must build a relationship with those individuals and make them experience how significant *they are* to you. You don't have to be creepy. You don't have to walk up to a stranger with a group of dancers moving around you, singing, "Significant moment...significant moment" while you say "hi." Instead, you could start by just learning an individual's name – how rare is that? Park had dozens of teachers during his high school career. The reason he remembers his Spanish teacher is that she made him feel significant from the start, learning his name. When Park entered her classroom for the first time, she shook each and every single hand of each student. She walked right up to Park and said, "What is your name?" Park replied, "My name is Richard Parkhouse." She exclaimed, "NO! No, señor! You are now Casa Parque" (Spanish for "Park House"). While this introduction was a bit silly, it started the relationship with significance: not only did she know his name, but she would remember his name.

You've often heard that "first impressions are the most important impressions." In terms of building a relationship with another person that is designed to help him or her be a better human being, eye contact, smiles, and a lack of body odor is a good start, but it's not everything that you need to make it a significant impression. You have to be brave: You have to go beyond the handshake and "hello," making your meeting a memorable moment. Your energy, your way of speaking, your attention to details, and your signals that you *actually* care about this human being will make the moment memorable. Even better, if you know anything about the person ahead of time – especially something notable or positive about the individual – that could assist you in building a starting point for the relationship. Regardless, begin the relationship as if it were not something that was only going to last a single conversation. What if you treated every interaction you had with every student on campus as if it were the start of a four-year friendship with potential for a lifelong impact?

Details matter. Your ability to be "in the details" matters. If you get to know someone, using details from his or her life that you have come to know over some time, you're more able to change that person's life for the better. It's like being a coach who is working to build the unique abilities of each of his or her players. This coach does not treat everyone *exactly* the same. He or she caters to the individual needs of each player. For example, Park's coach, John, took great care in knowing at what aspects of the game of baseball Park was excellent, acceptable, and needing significant development. "Coach" did not treat every player the same way in every situation: He was individually mentoring each player to be the best player in the best position he or she could be. That's your role as a teacher: to discover the details about what makes each person great, maximizing the chances for him or her to show that greatness, and to develop that person in those areas that need improvement. That starts with a memorable meeting, continues through the building of significant moments, and culminates with your "student" being placed on stage to celebrate the ways in which he or she has grown. If you don't care about getting to know a person for the long term, this is simply not possible. A special type of relationship is required. You are not finding more acquaintances to add to your list of people you act like you "know." You are building long-term, deep relationships that matter with others.

Is your purpose in the leadership class just to be a poster painter or balloon blower-upper? We have the feeling that if you are reading this text right now, you are desiring or being called to a greater role. Of the many roles that you will occupy as a student leader, that of "teacher" is one of the most profound. Further, your understanding of who is a teacher and how you can celebrate the role of teachers will further enable you to live out this role as a student leader at your school. Let's examine the attributes and roles of teachers.

What Is a Teacher?

No one in life gets anywhere without a teacher – no one. Teachers don't necessarily carry the title "teacher" or work in schools. They don't always have degrees that make them a teacher. In fact, most "teachers" in the sense we are discussing have professional qualifications that don't always relate to the field of education. Teachers are guides, confidants, and mentors: people who assist others forward. Teachers have many qualities that you should acknowledge and take up as your own as a student leader. First, teachers inspire. By "inspire," we mean that teachers, in any form, ignite curiosity. Teachers inspire those they serve to be open and desiring of further understanding about reality, a particular topic, and beyond. For example, it's through the inspiration of a teacher that you may become interested in a new subject matter. It's through a teacher that you may be interested in discovering more about yourself. Consider: In what ways have your teachers inspired you toward becoming your World's Greatest Me? In what ways will you inspire others through your actions and attitude?

Second, teachers acknowledge. Think about the ways that teachers have pointed out the ways that you have grown through your hard work. Have you ever had someone like a teacher show you an area in which you have significantly developed yourself? "Acknowledgement" comes in many forms. One could say kind words. One could help another see personal accomplishment or growth. One could create a moment where others get to see how another has advanced, even under difficult circumstances. You could acknowledge another student in your class – "You superstar, you" – as he or she turned in another piece of work to the instructor. You could acknowledge the ways in which your team members helped or grew during a recent campaign or project. You could acknowledge when one of your team leaders or instructors fulfilled a commitment or provided an excellent talk or lesson. Your words matter. Use them for good. Use them to build, not tear down.

Third, teachers take action. How many times have you seen a problem at your school and thought, "As much as that may be important, it's not my problem"? True teachers, and true student leaders, don't leave anything to be dealt with by someone else without being involved in some way themselves (even if they are simply the person notifying another of an issue). If you are the person recognizing a need, it's up to you to make the decision to take action, help others take action, or take no action at all; regardless, it's your decision. Teachers will take actions to assist or find others who are able to assist. How many times could the great teachers in your life have simply ignored you? They had many things to do, after all. Instead of ignoring you, they took notice, made you a priority, and took action. Who or what have you been ignoring around you? What cannot be left alone anymore?

Fourth, teachers believe. True teachers are not masters of sarcasm, cynicism, and negativity. Instead, with each and every interaction with their "students," they communicate a sense that they believe in what's possible. Your teacher believes in you. As a teacher, you show your belief in others. Pause for a moment and consider what it feels like to be believed in. Think about that. What does it feel like to know that another human being has faith that you can and probably will do great things? Does it feel like you are more able to be the

World's Greatest Me you can be because another human being believes it too? When a teacher believes that you can meet a challenge, you are more able to meet that challenge. Will you do that for another human being on your campus? Will you communicate your belief in others for them to be better today than yesterday?

Fifth, teachers care. Teachers are emotionally invested in those whom they serve. As a student leader, do you look at the hordes of younger and older students at your school with apathy and a lack of caring? Are you doing this simply to pad your résumé and look better on college applications? Chances are, you are a student leader because, somewhere inside of you, you have a positive regard for other human beings. You feel that assisting others is good and that others can be made better by your actions. More than that, you may actually care about how the people around you turn out or end up. Your caring is greatly empowering for others. It's through your care that you are motivated to notice the needs of others. It's through your emotional investment that you are willing to work hard to help another. As a teacher, allow your care for others to show. Don't hide it.

Sixth, teachers challenge their students. Have you ever had a class so easy that it nearly bored you to tears? Would you say that teacher was a great teacher? Have you had other educators who significantly challenged you to do better and better, working you through quite difficult circumstances? Would you say that these were great teachers? Strangely enough, the best teachers in our lives are those who have made us work the most. There is something special about someone who challenges us, because it's through the difficulty that we are able to grow. In what ways do you need to hold others accountable around you? In what ways do you need to make your way of working with them more urgent and important? Challenge others.

Finally, through all of this, teachers encourage. Teachers recognize that students are struggling and provide reassurance that success is not only possible but also probable with great amounts of hard work. In what ways are you providing a challenge and the encouraging words to back up your team? How are you counseling others around you through their most difficult times so that they can become their best selves more and more each day? Those whom you serve are looking to you to help them through the dark times so that they can emerge from these difficult periods better than ever before. You can help someone personally transform by encouraging him or her to press onward, even when it's difficult to do so.

How Can I Be a Teacher?

Teachers have a profound level of power. Teachers, themselves, are the starting point from which everything at your school happens. Without teachers, there is no school. Expanding your traditional definition of "teachers" to include everyone on your campus who mentors and teaches, you too have a profound level of power. You are part of this place called school that allows other human beings to become their personal best. Are you currently living like you have this level of importance in the lives of others? How can you live up to this calling? First, you, yourself, must make a personal commitment to work each day to be your personal best – one step better than the day before. It's from this standpoint that you are able to help others who are taking this same journey. Second, because you and your fellow student leaders have made this commitment individually, you can go out and do this brand of work together with one another. Because you are operating with a team of individuals rather than by yourself, so much is possible. Finally, as a team, you can go out and assist each and every person on your campus toward their personal best by creating significant moments for others. However, it all begins with you making the commitment to work each day to be your personal best. From there, here are five steps you can take to be a teacher to those whom you serve.

Share Your Story

Every person has a life story: a story about where you are from, where you are today, and where you are going. Though your story may not start deep in a rain forest, at the top of some magical mountain, or in a strange land (perhaps it does), the person who you are today began at some point in the past. You've grown into who you are today. You are heading somewhere. When you share your story with others, you are building a relationship with them. Your story provides the basis for others to be part of your journey. They see that they are characters in the unfolding tale called "you." Further, when you share your story, it opens up the opportunity for others to share their stories with you. You become part of their world as well. The sharing of stories has a deep root within humanity. We've been sharing our stories for a very, very long time as a human kind. If you want to be a teacher, you need to share your story so that others can learn from it and so that they can invite you to be part of theirs.

Create Opportunities for Others to Grow

You'll find in your student leadership class many times when it would be much easier for you to complete a task on your own. The assumption is that it would be much more trouble to allow another person to be part of the activity. It might take more time. It might involve difficult conversations. It might require that you make sacrifices, share power, or teach someone something. What do you give up when you go rogue like this? Chiefly, you don't provide the conditions that are required for learning, because you are robbing others around you of the opportunity to learn or refine a skill. In situations where you find yourself running to complete a task that you can easily complete on your own, consider asking another one of your team members to take part. Provide the soil from which others can grow. You are a capable person, but you'll be an even better team member if you create opportunities for others to learn. You'll never be able to ride a bike without pedaling. You have to get on the bike to be in the position to fail, learn, and try again. Without first steps, there are no further steps.

Create Opportunities to Stretch Others

How many times do you decide to "play nice" in your

leadership team, meanwhile being exceedingly frustrated by the lack of performance of another team member? Do you hold secret grudges against others on your team? Do you have a culture of growth within your leadership team where you converse about how things can be, how things are, and how things were? Before the next campaign, event, rally, etc., talk about the expectations for how each and every team member will advance his or her skills. Talk about how each person will raise his or her game to a new level while working with the rest of the team. As you are engaged in that activity, have continual conversations about how you are seeing other people living up to the promises they made before the event. Afterwards, have an open conversation about what went well and how others can improve. You should ask, "Do you believe in the purpose of this student leadership team?" Unless you are creating opportunities for others to be stretched and unless you are having conversations about what has been learned, you're not teaching. Create opportunities to stretch your team members.

Create Significant Moments for Others

At some point in your life, you're able to look back at a moment and learn something from it. Perhaps you had a friendship or relationship that had a profound impact upon you. Looking back on the person or people involved, you may be able to pull out a distinct lesson that you learned from them. Think back to a significant moment in your past involving another person. How did that person help you in learning an important lesson about life? Did this moment help shape you into the person who you are today? Moments like these do not have to be accidental. You can actually create them for other people. As a teacher, you can manufacture impactful moments for specific people. The more you know about what makes a person tick, what personal preferences that person has, and what needs he or she has for life and growth, the more you can simply provide the person with exactly what you feel that he or she needs. This can be something as small as a "hello." It could be something as large as raising money to help someone go to a school event that he or she normally could not afford to attend. The possibilities are endless. You could create anything. Anything could happen as a result.

Create Situations for Exploring Greatness

As a teacher, you can also manufacture experiences wherein an individual can explore his or her greatness. As we've described before, situations like these offer people the chance to be one step better than the day before (their personal best). To create a situation wherein one can explore his or her greatness, provide the individual with the opportunity to work on being his or her World's Greatest Me. This works best when an individual has an affinity for a specific activity. Get that person engaged in that activity. Help this individual see how much he or she has advanced in the past doing this activity. Assist this person in recognizing how he or she is performing in that activity today. Further, help the individual see new possibilities for how he or she could perform in this activity in the future. As a teacher, this is the most powerful tool that you have at your disposal. In situations such as these, students are engaging in an activity that they love. They have a chance to grow in that activity. They have a chance to propel their lives into unknown future possibilities through this activity. When one is exploring his or her greatness, he or she is laying the foundation for the passions, interests, and callings that will be with that person the rest of his or her life. If you failed to provide someone with the opportunity to explore his or her greatness in ways such as this, it's possible that the person would not ever become the best that he or she could be. That's how vital you are to others: without you, they may not live out their calling.

Can I Really Be a Teacher?

In Park's office, he has a photo of his six-year-old self sitting on the front stoop of his elementary school. The schoolhouse makes him look like he was born in the 1800s or something. There sits a line of young kids gleefully smiling in black-and-white, overexposed photo stock. Behind that line of kids is his strong, peaceful-looking second-grade teacher looking at the camera, as if she were saying "hello" through sixty years of time passed. What makes the photograph so beautiful is the image of the teacher standing behind the nine-or-so students on the schoolhouse step. To think, each of these nine kids probably went on for a full life. Many of these people probably had children and grandchildren themselves. Each probably went to serve others each day in his or her work and home life. How many generations, how many tens of thousands of individuals were impacted by this one educator? Would their lives be the same without this teacher? How important are you, then, as a student leader at your school?

Imagine yourself standing at the back of high school graduation, knowing that each and every student sitting in the seats around you was impacted in some way because of your involvement with student leadership. As you imagine the faces of all those people whom you supported over the years of school and all the heartache that allowed them to sit in these chairs, consider where they would be without you. Consider what would happen if you did not give them your personal best each day. What would happen if you missed a chance to create a significant moment with one or more of these individuals? Would they still be sitting there? When you finally are handed your diploma at graduation, will you be able to say that you can walk away with no regrets? Did you and your teammates band together for the sake of all, helping as many as possible to be in these seats? Alternatively, did you and your team operate in such a way that did not help and may have hindered the ability of others to join you at graduation? Every day, so many people are so used to acting like they are the only people who have something to lose if they don't bring their best. Reality check: People are depending on you. Their very lives may depend on you. Do you have their back? Or should someone else be standing there to support them instead?

What stops us from taking our place as mentors and teachers? Are we afraid of looking foolish? Ten years from now, will you feel embarrassed about being the type of person who extended a hand and said "hello" to a new person? In twenty years, will you feel like you should not have taken a chance on building relationships with people to whom you would not normally speak? Do you feel like you don't have something to offer the other human beings at your school? A very real possibility is that you may reach the end of your high school career and, sitting at graduation, look around you at all the faces of the people there with you and realize, "I could have mattered more. I could have done more. I could have had more relationships and more impact with these fellow students." The worst consequence of your lack of action is that you may not have had a relationship critical to your development and the development of another human being; everyone missed out. Why not be willing to step up and be so important to another human being? What is the cost of regret?

Everyone has something to offer. At the base, one always can build a relationship. All that's required to be a teacher, at the start, is to pay attention to the other people around you. Rather than taking them for granted, you notice their likes, dislikes, troubles, challenges, aspirations – anything that allows you to understand them more as individuals. From there, you are able to speak and interact with them in the ways that are most helpful. You can start to provide them with the words and attention in the ways that they need them most. Further, you can start to assist them in discovering what their personal best looks like each day. You can recognize them for trying something new, reaching a new level of performance, or for having a win. You can provide them with challenges that help them stretch and become even greater iterations of their personal best. However, it all starts with a first meeting and an ever-growing relationship.

How Do I Treat Teachers?

The ways in which you honor teachers at your school – whether they are in charge of classrooms, running the lunch rooms, sitting as members of your student leadership team, or are students simply walking the halls – have a profound impact upon the work of these teachers to continue and thrive. The best work of teachers often emerges where teaching is revered and honored. As a student leader, one of your many roles is to communicate the importance of teachers, celebrate the work of teachers who help create significant moments, and further strengthen the relationships between students and teachers.

How Do We Communicate the Importance of Teachers?

You can communicate the importance of teachers to students through the work of your student leadership class. At one graduation, every student's name was displayed on a huge marquee, alongside the name of his or her most inspirational teacher. At another rally, students who were inducted into the school's hall of fame had their most inspirational teacher's name below theirs. In both of these instances, students helped students communicate the importance of teachers. They did so by providing students with the chance to name those teachers who had the greatest impact upon them. Other students were able to recognize the role that these teachers played in their being the best they could be. How could you help students see the importance of teachers?

You can bring attention to teachers who have led winning teams of all kinds to victory. You can put a poster on the door of a teacher's classroom that lists those students who said this was their most inspirational teacher the week, semester, or year before. You can construct a "Wall of Heroes," including photos of the teachers, the places where they went to school, the number of years they have taught, and the approximate number of students whom they have helped graduate.

You can encourage athletes to deliver their jerseys to their most inspirational teachers the day before a game and say, "Mr. So-and-so, you are my most inspirational teacher; would you be willing to come to the game tomorrow wearing my jersey?" You can ask students at the start of a drama performance to recognize those teachers in the audience who have had an impact on them during their school career. You can provide the ways by which students can personalize letters, cards, and other gifts for teachers that have deep sentimental value.

How Do We Celebrate Significant Moments?
On your campus each day, there are potentially

hundreds of instances where teachers have been involved in significant moments that will change the lives and impact the futures of the students involved. Perhaps a student delivered his or her best presentation to date. Maybe a student was able to gain university acceptance. It's possible that a student may have significantly raised his or her grade point average. Moments like these often come and go without much fanfare. Your school could recognize significant moments like these and the students involved. That's a starting point. However, how much more impactful would that celebration be if you also recognized the ways in which teachers were involved in these significant moments?

What we celebrate is what we value. If you truly value teachers (whether they are fourteen years old or fifty years old), then they will have a large presence in those things that you celebrate at your school. If you don't celebrate much, it's arguable that you don't value much. If you celebrate the football team but don't take the time to celebrate your soccer team, your coaches, the teachers of the students, the parents of the players, etc., then it's possible that you value the football team more than you value everyone else. If you value teachers, it's up to you to actually show that. Without evidence, it's possible you don't value teachers.

How Do We Strengthen Relationships?

Most students are not taught how to regard their teachers. Frankly, most teachers are not trained in how to create an environment where others properly interact with them in the real world of your school. You have to train students how to build relationships with their teachers. You have to train teachers how to build relationships with their students. Without training them and without creating the circumstances in which relationships can be built between students and teachers, you are simply hoping that relationships like these will spring forth. That's mediocre at best. It's up to you to build up teachers and promote the ways in which students and teachers can interact with one another for mutual benefit.

How Can I Build Up Teachers?

Thank a teacher. How often each day do you thank other human beings for the integral part they are playing in your becoming healthier, happier, and wealthier? How often do you suppose that teachers of any kind are thanked for the work that they are doing. Whether they are coaches, students, mentors, formal classroom teachers, administrators, principals, or kids down the hall who have been helping you, they all may go the entirety of today without anyone thanking them for being an important part of their lives. When you thank someone, you are telling the person that he or she is valued.

Celebrate a teacher. As we said earlier, you celebrate what you value. Not only does the work of teachers often go without thanks, but it's rarely celebrated. A celebration is the byproduct of something important happening. Call "time out" and celebrate your culture. Celebrate your belief that no one gets anywhere without a teacher. When something notable happens that is worth positive regard, a celebration could spring up. How often do you and your school notice when something important happens and celebrate it? The first step is to notice. Then, you can party.

Bring a teacher into an existing celebration. When something is already happening, like a rally, drama performance, sports game, competition, or any other campus activity, use that as an opportunity to showcase the ways in which teachers have helped the students there. Rather than simply going about the business of the event, where only a handful of people may be the focus, expand the focus to include others, including teachers.

Overall, these steps all involve the act of recognizing teachers. Here is the quintessential formula for recognizing a teacher of any kind.

The Four Keys of Recognizing a Teacher

First, use the word "inspirational." Words like "favorite" and "best" often denote shallow popularity. While these words may be hints of good things going on, "inspirational" shows that the teacher is not just a nice guy or gal – this teacher is a person who has made this student more likely to pursue living as his or her personal best. Of all the words that could be used, inspirational most accurately hits the mark.

Second, use the word "impact." Describe the ways in which the teacher has impacted the student's life and potentially changed his or her future as a result. It's one thing to say, "You inspire me," or "You are my most inspirational teacher." It's another to say these things in addition to providing the teacher with the story of how he or she impacted you. As a team, take the time to allow students to tell their teachers how they have impacted their lives.

Third, say "thank you." Oddly enough, time and time again, we've seen so many amazing moments between students and teachers where a "thank you" is not exchanged. A "thank you" says that the student is grateful for the teacher's involvement in his or her life. It's one of the most fundamental exchanges between grateful human beings. Ensure that you model thank yous when recognizing teachers.

Finally, the ultimate step, invite the teacher to be part of a larger celebration later on, such as a rally, performance, or competition, and publicly recognize him or her. It's in this exchange that a grand significant moment can be created, where others can see the ways in which this teacher impacted the students and where others can see the important relationship between students and teachers.

Summary

In the end, recognize that relationships are the starting point of everything you do as a student leader. They are the basis for your ability to optimally learn here at this school. Relationships are the foundation from which your leadership team can assist others. Further, relationships are the foundation for the work of teachers to change lives and impact futures. Consider how Chris was impacted by his teachers before and after the summer of his junior year. Early on, even when he was a young boy, his teachers provided him with the basis from which he could do so well after his injury. After his injury, many teachers came forward to assist him. Teachers can make or break an individual. What type of teacher will you be to those around you?

We thank our inspirational teachers for the parts they have played in our lives. We are so grateful to you for believing in us, even before we did. Thank you.

BLUEPRINT QUESTIONS:

1. Describe a friend, mentor, or teacher who helped you become the person you are today. What qualities of that person's character helped you most? Provide examples of three qualities and how they helped you.

2. Imagine the person who sits two seats behind you or three seats to your right or left in your student leadership class. What do you know about this person? What are five ways you could further build a relationship with him or her in the next two weeks?

3. What is your life story? What is your past? What is your present? What is your future? Where are you going? How have teachers played a part in each step?

DARES:

1. On your own, find one person on campus who

you do not know and introduce yourself to him or her. Ask this person what he or she is interested in.

2. As a student leadership team, discuss: How will you inspire, acknowledge, take action with, believe in, care about, challenge, and encourage one group of individuals on campus next week? Manufacture mini-experiences to accomplish this. Every action you take must be personal and face-to-face.

3. Share your life story with one person this week on your student leadership team.

4. On your own, take the four steps above to recognize one teacher in your life this week.

CHAPTER EIGHT

ALL STUDENTS ARE GIFTED AND TALENTED

"Self-awareness of your gifts, talents, skills, and weaknesses is the starting point of you becoming your World's Greatest Me."

Most of the doctors and nurses with whom Chris interacted did not believe that he was going to have much ability to move his arms and legs in the future. While he was expected to recover a small amount of upper body strength, it was expected that he would have limited leg movement. Time and time again, he found himself explaining to doctors and rehabilitation specialists that he was gaining more strength in his arms and legs than they were saying was possible. Often, he was met with disbelief – that is, they often downplayed the likelihood that he was experiencing that which he was claiming. Ironically, it was those with little or no medical knowledge who had the greatest belief in Chris's abilities. For example, when he attended a summer camp in Rhode Island for paraplegics, most of the staff there had no medical knowledge and simply were giving their time to help people build wheelchair skills, cope with emotional challenges, and help build muscle strength. A common skill that many people in wheelchairs learn is how to do a wheelie up a curb. Staff with medical training did not believe that it was possible for Chris to do this exercise. Chris would often say, "Why? I can't do this? Come on! Tell me why!" It was the staff with no medical training who had not been indoctrinated in these beliefs. They had the open hope and expectation that Chris could accomplish whatever he set his mind to. With their help, Chris quickly developed the ability to do wheelies up curbs – something doctors, nurses, and medically trained rehabilitation specialists said was impossible. Chris was allowed, enabled, and encouraged to develop his unique skills. He got to set his goals in instances such as these. He began to wonder if he would, despite what doctors said, be able to walk again. He believed in his skills. He worked to develop them.

Not everyone is the same. Not everyone has the same goal. If you look around at everyone in your student leadership class, you'll see many different skills and a great lack of skill. One could look at those who are missing certain skills and say, "Wow, you really don't belong here. You're not up to this leadership thing."

However, a true "leadership mind" recognizes that each and every person brings something unique and of value into the school – whether he or she is in the leadership class or not, whether he or she has the best grades or not, whether he or she is "doing well" by the most popular ways of measuring success at your school or not. One of the values of the World's Greatest High School is "all students are gifted and talented." You have your own set of gifts, talents, and skills. These gifts, talents, and skills are part of what make you *you*. If each and every person at your school had the opportunity to shine using these gifts and talents, your school would be an exceedingly different place, because people would be largely defined by their growing successes. What would it look like to build a school each day where each person could work on bettering him- or herself in his or her unique gifts, talents, and skills? This would be the World's Greatest High School.

Unfortunately, usually in schools, the focus is on the "top" gifted and talented students or the students experiencing the greatest challenges. If you are not part of the 35 or so students of your year doing the best or the bottom 45 doing the worst, not much focus may be placed on your unique gifts, talents, and skills and how to build those up. One group that is often emphasized is the top group academically or athletically. Another group is the students experiencing severe challenges in their lives that often cause them to act out, drop out, or end up in the office. If you take time as a leadership class to step back and really think about others and really take a look at everyone on your campus, you can see that each and every person possesses some type of greatness in the form of these unique gifts and talents. If we think of greatness in those terms, everyone possesses greatness. Your job as student leaders, then, is to create spotlights for greatness everywhere: on every student, including those who are not at the "top" or the "bottom" of your school's measure of performance.

Self-Awareness

Take a look at your own gifts, talents, and skills. Often, it's difficult for a person to look at anything he or she does and have enough self-awareness (especially when the person is a teenager) to say, "I am really good at A, and I need to grow in XYZ ways." If you can do that, that's quite an advanced move! Even more advanced is the ability to examine oneself and say, "My personal disadvantages are ABC, and so I need to get some assistance from others who have talents in these areas." For all the skills that are taught in school and in life, one that is rarely grasped until a much older age (if ever) is "self-awareness." Self-awareness is, in part, the intimate knowledge of what one is capable of doing, what one is less capable of doing, and what one must do to better him- or herself. It's an amazing thing to consider that so many people walk throughout their day not knowing what is going on inside of them, not knowing how they are doing moment to moment, until a moment hits them in the face and screams, "Life is hard," "I failed a test," or "I'm alone." It's like having a dear friend who suddenly says, "I can't be friends with you anymore because I'm so angry at you," never seeing the signs of a problem brewing in the relationship until it was too late. How often do we do this exact thing with ourselves? Often, people don't know how well things are going until things are not going well. Sometimes, people don't know how bad things are until they get a small dose of the good life. Self-awareness is perhaps the greatest skill you can master as a student leader and as a human being. It's through this skill that you can discover who you are and what you are capable of doing. Also, it's through self-awareness that you are able to see what you are less capable of doing.

How do you regard weakness? For most student leaders, the way that they discover their gifts and talents comes from the following pattern of thought: "If things are going well in a certain area of my life, that may be my talent; where things are not going well, that's probably my weakness." However, weakness is often treated as a secret. After all, would you be comfortable broadcasting your personal weaknesses inside of any class at this school? The ideal situation, especially for student leaders, is that they can accept that they have talents and weaknesses. They are comfortable with those weaknesses, like the way one is accepting of a friend who is a good person but is still working things out. If you can look at your own weaknesses in this way, you are able to accept that you are how you are today, but tomorrow may be a different story. Tomorrow, you could advance in those weaknesses. You could obtain assistance from others around you who have talents in these areas of personal need. Your weaknesses don't necessarily have to be a secret; they are part of what has allowed your gifts and talents to emerge. Who would you be, after all, without these weaknesses? You would be someone else! Know your weaknesses and respect them. Take time to get to know them. Work with your weaknesses to build a better tomorrow. Your weaknesses are as important as your strengths.

Self-awareness of your gifts, talents, skills, and weaknesses is the starting point of you becoming your World's Greatest Me. At this starting point, you can answer for yourself, "What am I capable of doing? What am I *most* capable of doing? Where do I need help?" It's through this honesty with yourself that you are able to better your gifts, talents, and skills while addressing and minding your weaknesses. Further, you are able to be a better member of your student leadership team, because you know what and how you can give your best personal contribution. For example, through self-awareness, you may know that you have a talent for staying organized but don't have a great talent for getting a group to do what you ask. Accordingly, you may choose to work with the leader of your small group or committee to help him or her stay organized. Conversely, you may have a great gift and talent of communicating with large groups, letting them know what is going on and what direction the team will be taking, and exciting others about what's next. However, you may not be good at coaching individual team members who are not performing to their potential. You may lead the group, but you may have another person take responsibility for helping other team members when they are struggling. It's through your self-awareness, by being aware of your strengths and not hiding from your weaknesses, that you are able to be your World's Greatest Me today. It's through great self-awareness that you can stop being someone who you are not and develop comfort in your skin: You can grow in your talents and mind your weaknesses.

One of our great teachers said that the most important friend you can have is yourself. It's highly possible that we are far more likely to recognize the talents and accept the faults of one of our friends, more than we know our own strengths and are willing to respect where we need to grow. It's not easy being a friend to yourself. Being a friend to yourself requires that you look into your own thoughts and actions, even when it's not comfortable. Further, it requires that you take a nearly unthinkable step: to accept where you are today so that there's the possibility of doing better tomorrow. So often, one is so scared by his or her weaknesses that he or she despises a situation that makes him or her feel that weakness. What would it be like to be fully aware of one's gifts, talents, skills, and weaknesses and also be fully accepting of them? As a student leader at the World's Greatest High School, you can't simply make a promise to do better tomorrow; you must see where you are today first. Then, you can accurately know what must be better tomorrow. Know yourself so that you can accept yourself so that you can grow.

My Personal Best

Being self-aware like this can be quite exciting. It's an adventure. Because you know about your gifts, talents, skills, and weaknesses, you have the chance to step back and consider each day as a huge opportunity. "This day," you might say, "is an opportunity for me to be the World's Greatest Me I can be." Your self-awareness can be the ground on which you can challenge yourself to be one step better than the day before. Think about that. If today is the opportunity to be the best you ever, what does that mean? What does that offer you? What sorts of opportunities do you have today to be that best you? Truly, today is the best chance for you to be the best you ever on the face of this Earth. That's an enthralling experience: "Regardless of anything that happens today," you might think, "I'll be the best me that I can be." However, this is not easy. It's so tempting to fall into that Mediocre High (also known as "Mediocre Me") way of thinking that says, "I'm okay being okay today. Today will be okay. Hopefully tomorrow will be okay too." It's easy to simply allow the day's events and the emotions of others around you to tell you the type of day you are having. This is "easier" in a sense, because it does not require that you do anything different. Further, at your worst, you could fall into the trap of believing that there is no way to better your personal situation. You could fall into the No Hope mentality that says that nothing could or should be done to change a thing. This destructive way of thinking often says, "Things have always been this way, and they probably will always be this way." This shuts off the chance for anything better to happen. Instead, you, your leadership team, and your school should build up a place that proudly proclaims that "this is the school where you can become your personal best." It's not that you are trying to be other people's personal best – this is the place where YOU can be YOUR personal best.

With self-awareness, you can see what's within your grasp today and potentially tomorrow and the days after. How many times do you hear people say, "You can be anything you want to be"? There are some things that are in your grasp today and some things that may be within reach in the days to come. However, we have to be realistic about our gifts and talents and the potential for those gifts and talents in the future. Your self-awareness allows you to see what's possible and what is not. If you want to be an astronaut but don't want to do any work in math or science, then you need to be realistic and see that space travel may not be within your reach. If you want to be one of the world's greatest jockeys (who are usually about five feet tall) and you are almost seven feet tall, then your self-awareness can inform you that your dream may need to be adjusted. Do you have the ability to ride horses? Absolutely! Will you be able to ride in the Kentucky Derby? Most likely not. If you are seven feet tall, you have a better chance to play professional basketball than ride in the Kentucky Derby. Beware of situations that say, "All I have to do is believe in myself, and I can do anything I want." You have to be keenly aware of how much work is required of you to undertake any goal. You have to be knowledgeable of where you need to grow. Your belief in yourself is greatly important, but even more important is your ability to see where you are today and what you need to do to make yourself the best you that you possibly can be *today*. It's through this sort of reflection that each day can begin with you saying, "Where am I now? What's one thing (or more) that I can do today to make that better? If I keep doing this, how far could I go?" Your personal best is what you can do today. You may have a dream for the future, but it's today that's in your hands. If you're not willing to work hard today on what is in front of you, then what makes you think the future will be any different?

Each day, you have the chance to further develop your gifts, talents, and skills. You can't go to the store and buy these. You could go to the "challenge store" and work hard to get better one day at a time in these gifts and talents. What if there were such a store in your neighborhood, where you could walk in and say, "I want to get better at being a better speaker as a leader," and some dude would say, "GREAT! We have just the thing for you!" and was able to hand you a set of challenges to undertake throughout the day? What if you knew that if you kept going to this store, you would get closer than ever to your dreams and aspirations? Would you keep going? Would you enjoy going each day? If you have not guessed where we're going with this already, this place called "school" can be your challenge store. You can't go anywhere to receive your gifts, talents, and skills. Instead, you need to go places that will allow you to further develop these. Is your school such a place where you can truly develop your unique gifts? Is this the type of place that would allow other people around you to also better theirs? This is what you are being asked to do as a student leader: create the conditions for growth and life where each and every person at your school can become their personal best each day. However, you can't transform the school without first transforming yourself. You can't expect your student leadership team, teachers, or administrators to build the type of school that can challenge you each day without you being the type of person who is willing to take up and conquer such a challenge. School transformation only follows personal transformation.

Put yourself in situations where you can explore your greatness. Today, you could say to yourself, "I'm going to try to uncover a gift or skill that I didn't know that I have." Perhaps you have the feeling that you're going to work toward becoming the best piano player you can be. Maybe you want to be the world's greatest plumber. Regardless, it starts with your willingness to be challenged and to explore what it feels like to do better and to work harder than you ever have before. Today, you probably, based upon what you already know about yourself, have some idea about what you want to become in life. You may not know for sure what you'll end up being, but because of your gifts, talents, and skills today, you have a good idea of what you could become. However, you're probably not going to be able to get there or be that thing tomorrow; there is a long, difficult journey ahead. You can't walk the whole journey today. Instead, you can only walk today's part of that journey. In fact, you can only really walk the part of this journey that is under your feet right now as you read this book. Each step you take is important for exploring your greatness and for uncovering your gifts and talents. So, today, when a challenging situation arises, that's going to be the chance you have to better yourself. That's going to be the opportunity for you to be the best you in that moment. Will you rise to that challenge and be willing to be part of it? Will you withdraw and hide from the chance to take a risk? Will you place yourself in a situation that could feel uncomfortable but that you know will help you forward in your journey? You have to make this decision in each moment of today. Every breath offers you the chance to step up or back away. Which will you choose? Your personal best, your World's Greatest Me, is not some destination at the top of some hill somewhere with beams of light shooting from it. Instead, your personal best is what you can do right now that is one iota better than the moment or day before. Right now, you can be your best you.

Do Something You've Never Done Before

You often don't know you have a talent until you try. Think back to your youth when you were involved (if you were) in youth sports. It's possible that you played one, two, or three seasons of the sport before you realized, "Hmm, I don't feel like I'm having fun doing this. I'm just not becoming a better player. This does not feel like it is for me." Then, sometime after, you moved onto another sport, and you suddenly discovered that you enjoyed it and you were quite good at it. So many people have experienced a situation just like this. It's when we break from our comfortable routine and attempt something that we have never tried before that we often find ourselves more happy, fulfilled, and challenged. As a teenager, this is one of the prime times of life to put yourself in situations that allow you to find out what gifts you possess. How many times have you heard of a person going to college, only to realize that he or she was studying the wrong subject? Had that person explored that subject and other areas of interest earlier, would he or she have been required to go through that mid-university change? Probably not. Imagine if any of the great people of this century stuck to what did not challenge or engage them. Would they have become the great people they turned out to be?

It's up to you to help others take these first steps into undiscovered talents. It's like the leadership student who was asked by his class president to do the opening inspirational talk for the class the following day. This leadership student had never done a presentation in front of the class before, and he was feeling quite insecure about it. Not only did his class president provide him with this opportunity to grow, but she also reminded him that this was a chance for him to do something that he never had done before. Because this student had made a commitment to explore his greatness daily in the leadership class, he willingly took on the challenge, put together the presentation, and was supported by his leadership team as he took these first steps in this challenge. He rose to the challenge and discovered that, though he was a bit scared, he greatly enjoyed talking in front of large groups. It's possible that he would have never discovered this if it were not for a member of his leadership team challenging him to try something he had never tried before.

Here are some ways to develop your gifts, talents, and skills as well as those of others.

First-Step Mentality

Support others as they take their first steps in a new challenge. Thinking back to the first steps we mentioned before, you may be like us: We don't remember our first steps, but we can imagine what it was like for others around us. When a baby takes his or her first steps, what do people do as the baby wobbly stands and begins to put one foot in front of the other? Often, they get wide eyed and say, "Oh! Look at my baby! Such a great thing! Look at him or her take his or her first steps! Keep going! You can do it!" Everybody around is excited, and they applaud the attempt. From there, a mentor steps up and helps the baby with future steps over and over again. There is no doubt that the child will fall down again and again, but with a mentor there to support the attempts, the baby is more likely to make progress toward the goal of walking and feel safe and supported in making further attempts. As a student leader, you should adopt this way of approaching challenges. First, on your own behalf, you should accept that falling down is part of learning new skills. You should expect that things will not always go smoothly and that you'll experience great challenges along the path of your learning. Second, you should be there for others as they make their first and subsequent attempts at a new challenge. You can be the mentor who supports your friends or fellow students in becoming their personal best. No matter what, you can maintain the perspective that learning is step-by-step: left foot, right foot, left, right, until the motion simply becomes natural. That's how you experience greatness: by taking challenging steps.

However, this way of thinking is not the norm. Somewhere along the way in life, it became acceptable for some to criticize the first steps of others. When students are taking their first steps in high schools throughout the country, they are subject to being shamed, bullied, and rejected, simply because they are trying something new. If kids learned how to walk for the first time when they were teenagers and schools were as they are in many places today, these kids may decide to not walk at all out of fear of being ridiculed. So, while we can talk about how you can look at your own first steps and how you can look at the steps of others around you, one of the greatest challenges you can undertake as a student leader is building the kind of school where first steps are not only safe to take but are celebrated as well. The school as a whole, in the most ideal situation, must agree that this is the place where people get to explore their greatness, and that involves failure. In such a school, the community agrees that their greatest calling is to give each and every person that which is needed for them to thrive, including the challenges to help them grow and the respect for the process of failing and, eventually, succeeding. Today, this may not be the situation at your school.

Stretch Yourself

As their name implies, first steps are simply *first steps*. What about everything that happens after? After you've taken your first steps in a certain challenge, you need to push and stretch to the next level, and then to the next level, and then to the next. As you keep stretching and pushing, you'll get closer and closer to what you might call "mastery." Today, if you did nothing new – if you simply did today as you have always done in days past – what's the possibility that you would grow as a result of this? If at all, very little. It's like the college baseball player who was playing in one of the best teams in the league. Nine times out of ten, he was playing teams that were significantly weaker than his. On days where his team was playing a particularly weak team, he would lower his guard and play a sloppier game. While his team still won, there was, for him, little challenge in the game. He never pushed himself because he did not feel like it was a necessity. After one game where he was not playing his strongest, the coach approached him and asked why he was playing such a weak game. The player explained that there was no point if there was no challenge. The coach, a bit angry, replied, "You are only going to find out something about yourself when you go up against the best. Challenge yourself every game by playing against the best *you*." On the most basic level, it's up to you to be your own coach and push yourself to stretch your ability, competing against your best self so that you can take yourself to the next level with each breath through each challenge.

Your student leadership class, your other classes, the hallways at your school – these all can be the training grounds for your personal best. You don't have to wait until college to live the good life. The good life may simply be living today as the best version of you alive.

Rather than waiting for some teacher to assign you something that will be the golden key to your future, treat every moment as if it were part of the workout that is building the muscles for the ultimate life you have been seeking. In this way, you can coach yourself. You can mentor yourself. At the same time, your student leadership team can help you stretch your abilities. If you are reading this far into this book, we imagine that you have committed to one another to explore your greatness together. Part of that commitment is helping others find new challenges to which they can rise. Further, your commitment to one another means that you will not allow your fellow team members to simply do what is required to be "okay." Instead, you hold each other to the moving standard that today can be better than yesterday. When someone is not living up to that commitment, it's time for a larger conversation that will enable each of your team members to better live up to your group's promise. While so much of your work will be alone, away from your team, the team can greatly support each person within it in stretching to the next level and beyond. Your team can have great power in accelerating your personal growth.

We Is Greater Than Me

In your student leadership team, it's part of your job to help others step back and identify their gifts, talents, and skills and help each of them advance these. In your student leadership class, you can help one another find out your abilities and identify those things that are hindering your progress. It's possible that weaknesses will be discovered along the way. Don't treat weaknesses like something shameful. It's possible that a weakness is simply not an aspect of yourself or others that you or they wish to develop. Not every student leader wants or needs to be a high-energy speaker in front of thousands of students. It's also possible that a weakness is simply a clue to where you or others need to further develop yourselves with the help of your team members. In these ways, consider weaknesses as something to be understood and respected; don't hide weaknesses, as they sometimes provide great clues about the potential for your personal best. This is "self-awareness" taken into the group setting. A successful leader can clearly define his or her abilities, disabilities, and weaknesses. An even more successful leader is one who can identify those in others and help others see these and grow. A successful group of leaders is one that can look at each group member and say, "I can see your gifts, talents, and skills; I can see your weaknesses; together, we can help one another be our personal best. Because we have different gifts and needs, we can support one another and be a stronger team." It's through this way of being as a group that you are able to communicate an authentic respect for one another.

If you are an older student, you may be reading this and thinking about many of the gifts, talents, and skills of the younger students on your leadership team. You may also be thinking about their weaknesses. What would happen if you acknowledged your mutual respect for these team members by saying, "I've noticed your gifts, and I see how you are working to become your personal best. I just want you to know that if you keep working like this, I could definitely see you as a great student body president" (or any other role). What would those younger students experience by having an older student, such as yourself, providing this type of acknowledgement? They would feel like someone knows who they are. They would see that someone recognizes them for their gifts and talents. They would realize that they have a potential mentor in this older student who could help them go to the next level. They would feel affirmed, confident, and wanted.

If you are a younger student, you might have recently joined the leadership team and have witnessed how they treat you and the other newer students. What would happen if you stood up right now (or at any appropriate time that would not get you in trouble) and said, "I just want to say that I feel like I'm very welcomed here. I can see how each of you brings some unique gifts and talents into this team. I need your help, because I want to become the best me that I can be. Would you help me by challenging me to do things that don't necessarily come easy for me?" It's possible that, as a younger student, you are not comfortable talking to others about what you are thankful for. Consider this a challenge for you to undertake to stretch yourself.

Celebration is not just about applauding others. When you recognize greatness in action, that's a chance for you to become involved and exercise your own skills. When you see greatness in action, call it out and celebrate it. Share words about the greatness that you witnessed, as an individual or as a whole team. Spotlight greatness within your class. Then, consider how you can use your own gifts and talents to help those other people stretch themselves and be challenged to reach that next level. It's like the fitness coach at the gym who helps his or her partner do one more push, one more rep, one more weight than the session before. By being a great mentor, this fitness coach is becoming a better weight lifter him- or herself. It's through recognizing others challenging themselves and helping them take the steps to do their personal best that you are able to be their mentor and exercise your gifts and talents. Celebration, then, is about recognizing, affirming, helping, and growing. Everyone benefits, not just the person being celebrated.

While you are most definitely capable of advancing your gifts, talents, and skills and able to work daily to be the best you, World's Greatest Student Leaders can help you accelerate your progress. Where it's hard to see where you, yourself, need to grow, your team is there to support you. Where you can offer support to others, you can grow by giving the best of your gifts, talents, and skills to support them. Your leadership team, and the work you do with your fellow student leaders, can be a way by which you can advance everyone within your class and beyond.

Seeing With New Eyes

Imagine for a moment that each person within your school, every person, is trying to be the best person that he or she can be. What if each of these people had certain gifts, talents, and skills unique to him or her?

What if he or she needed your help in developing those gifts so he or she could live the best life possible for him or her? Would you help that person? Right now on your campus, there are hundreds, if not thousands, of individuals who want to live the fullest, best lives imaginable. Many of these students will do okay if left to their own designs. However, with your involvement, they could live out their ultimate potential. Further, if they were to live out their lives as their personal best each day, even more people would be able to live a better life as a result. It's possible that not every person on your campus today is "trying" or working in the way that you think is best. The question we have for you is, "What are you going to do about it?" As a student leader, it's easy to look at those outside your classroom and accuse them of not having school spirit, being lazy, not caring, or just acting mean. That's the easiest thing you can do: blame other people for their own problems and act like it's not your business to help them do anything different. Chances are, if you took more time each day to get to know individuals whom you've never spoken with at length before, you'd discover that people need you and that you are able to help. Some student leaders will struggle to even speak to strangers. Others will speak to strangers and be challenged to know what to do to help them. Some leaders will struggle to keep up with the challenge of helping their fellow students each day. If you are reading this book, we want to believe that you already are seeing students with the eyes of your best you. Using those eyes, being the best you that you can be, what do you see about the people walking through the hallways each day? Do you see that they need your help? Do you see how you could potentially help them? Will you help them? You are part of this team so that you can and will help!

Start looking for the World's Greatest gifts, talents, and skills in each of your fellow students. Step up and create opportunities for others to demonstrate their greatness. Then, step back and watch. Imagine what it will be like to create the stage on which others can shine and be able to watch someone become a better human being because of your efforts. Imagine what it will be like to know that a person was more able to live his or her best life because you gave of yourself in this way. That's what leadership is all about: setting up other people to shine. Like Chris, you first must be your most loyal, faithful coach. Start by learning your strengths and weaknesses. Exercise those. Then, help others do the same.

BLUEPRINT QUESTIONS:

1. What do you enjoy doing? What do you know you are good at? At what do you know you are less skilled? Provide examples of each.

2. What gifts, talents, and skills do you want to develop in the next twenty-four hours? Provide examples of ways in which you will work on bettering those skills.

3. What are some ways in which your student leadership team discourages first steps or first

attempts? How could you and the team encourage these?

DARES:

1. On your own, within the next twenty-four hours, do something you've never tried before that you know will make you and your life better. Share your experiences with your student leadership team.

2. On your own, for the next twenty-four hours, act as if each person wants to do better but needs your help to do so. In at least three instances, provide assistance to another person, even if you do not know him or her, to help that person take steps to do better. Share your experiences with your student leadership team.

3. As a student leadership team, organize an event where you showcase others (not on your team) doing their world's greatest in their individual skills. Ensure that you include Kileys, Alyssas, Austins, and Camo Kids.

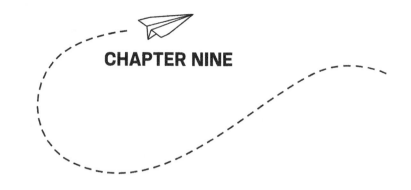

CHAPTER NINE

EVERY DAY IS AN OPPORTUNITY

"Right now, you have the opportunity to be the best you that you can be."

After nine months of intense healing, Chris returned to school his senior year while continuing his training and conditioning at a local rehabilitation center. Here, he worked with a man whom he regarded as the most amazing physical therapist that he had ever encountered. Dave was a therapist, mentor, and teacher who recognized that Chris was advancing further in his abilities than one in the medical field might traditionally expect. Chris had gifts and talents that he was developing that were unique to him. Dave did everything that he could to help Chris take on becoming the best man that he could be each day. Chris made the decision that he wanted to work his entire senior year to be able to walk across the stage at graduation – something that seemed impossible to those who did not believe in Chris. However, because Dave believed in Chris, they both worked toward this mammoth goal. Chris saw each meeting with Dave as an opportunity to work toward this goal. He would not be able to accomplish this feat in a matter of days. It would take him nearly the entire year to be able to do this. Chris began to research, learning that there existed braces that would support his entire body, allowing him to swing and move his legs on his own. However, he also learned that he would have to develop uncanny upper body strength that his doctors did not regard as within reach. He believed in his gifts. He had a mentor who was willing to help him. Every day, Chris worked toward this goal of developing enough strength to walk across the stage at the end of the school year in front of his classmates and his parents.

Every day is an opportunity for you to become your World's Greatest Me. Regardless of whether you are getting straight A's, are struggling, are lonely, are angry, or are doing fine, no matter who you are and how you're doing, today is a chance for you to be your personal best. Wherever you are right now reading this, take a moment to pause and take a few breaths. Seriously, stop and do that. Focus on the feeling of the air going in and out of your nose. Focus on the feeling of your lungs filling up and then expelling the air within. Feel how each breath is just one before another before another, on and on. Take this moment one breath at a time. Breathe like this for a moment.

(Please pause and breathe for a few moments.)

Today, right now, you have the opportunity to be the best you that you can be. So much of school is future oriented. If you ask many students in the hallway why they are here today, you'll get many answers. However, one that will come up time and time again is that they are here because they want to graduate; go to college, tech school, or the military; get a good job; and have the good life. Many times today at your school, students will be thinking about how low their grades are and how they may be in danger of being unable to have the future that they desire – whether that's graduation, some sort of educational or military experience afterwards, or having a family that is happy and proud of their accomplishments. Students will pack into counselors' offices to talk about the dangers of not making the grades. Students will have difficult conversations with their parents about their current and future grades in certain courses. These are all future concerns. So much of what the people around you will be focused upon is the future – a future about which they feel unsure and insecure. However, little focus will be placed upon that which they have the most control over. Few times will students, teachers, parents, and others take the steps in the one area that they can nearly guarantee success: today. Right now. You can't change your life five years from now, unless you have some sort of time machine. Fortunately, you can change your life today, right now. You can't study for your current math class ten years from now. However, you can better your situation in mathematics today. Today, you can't make friends with that person who sits next to you in the morning two years from now. However, you can take steps to build a relationship with that person today, right now. Put simply, this moment is the best time to be your personal best. Not tomorrow. Not after you graduate. Right now. What are you going to do, right now, about that? If you want to change your future, change today.

Take a moment to look at the cover of this book. You'll notice that weaving in and out of the text on the cover is a paper airplane. That paper airplane was not placed there by accident. It has great significance. Like you, that paper airplane is on a journey. If you imagine every student in your class going to the side of the room and throwing a paper airplane at the same time, all those planes would go in different directions for different distances. Not every plane takes the same path. If you think about the path of your paper airplane as your path to greatness, then you can't say that everyone will have the same journey. Not everyone will take the same path. You have a path that you will take to become your personal best. That's your path. It's exciting that you, alone, have this unique path in life. Your path is different from every other person's path. Our path is different from yours. Our paths may cross along our journeys, but we and you are headed different places. Your World's Greatest Me, your neighbor's World's Greatest Me, and your teacher's World's Greatest Me are all different. As a developing student leader, it's so important to remember that your travels toward your personal best will not look the same as others. The path and the destinations are not the same.

If you look at the way that your school as a whole

treats students, you may think that the school is under the delusion that everyone's path is the same. The school acts as if everyone is headed toward similar ends. The focus is not on greatness; it's on something else entirely. Everyone takes a similar sequence of courses to get the same diploma. While each student may do something unique with that diploma after graduation, the way in which the school is run, bell to bell, the way that teachers grade students, and the ways in which people are celebrated for their accomplishments may all make it seem like everyone is headed toward the same end goal and must take the same steps to get there. Your job as a student leader is not to say that the grading system needs to change or that class schedules need to change or that the requirements for graduation need to change (though you can definitely, kindly, suggest those things). Your job is to recognize and celebrate the manifestations of greatness that pop up in nearly every moment of every day with your fellow students. Your job is to create significant moments where each student feels seen, recognized, and supported in the unique ways for his or her unique path and potential destination. Your job is to intimately, uniquely construct the perfect place for all kinds of greatness to thrive at your school. The journeys are not the same, so you don't celebrate everyone the same. You don't create significant moments for others always with the same cookie cutter. You have to create significant moments and celebrations as if you knew that each person was a different human being, going in a different way, headed toward a different place. You have to create the kind of place where THEY can be the best THEM today.

Similar to previous chapters, let's discuss how you can put your goals and beliefs into play in three ways to create the kind of place that allows each person to be his or her World's Greatest Me each day. First, we'll talk about the "me" dimension. Then, we'll talk about how "me" can go to "we." Finally, we'll discuss how you and your leadership team can involve others as well.

World's Greatest Me

Each moment of today is an opportunity to be your World's Greatest Me. Since you were probably quite young, teacher after teacher has asked you to consider your personal goals for the future – a future that was decades away. Now, you're quite older and are still asked to visualize a future that may only be a handful of years away. Do you feel any more secure and sure about that future than you did when you were in elementary school? Have your plans changed over the years? Are you burnt out about long-term goal setting? We have noticed, more and more, a propensity for older students to be less and less excited about setting goals for the future than younger students. We've asked many students why this is and have observed many responses. However, most commonly, students agree that the long-term future feels much less in their hands than what's going on this year and next year. Most high school students we've spoke to, for example, say that they are far more interested in what's happening in their high school career than the destination that they have set for themselves afterwards. This was quite surprising for us to hear. Do you feel this same way? Do you feel like what's happening this year (and maybe next) is more important, exciting, and on your mind than what is going to happen five years from now? An explanation for this may be that what's happening this year *is* more important than what's going to happen years from now. We would go a step further and say that the most important thing that's happening in your life is not what's happening this year: The most important thing in your life is what's happening right now – *right now*.

This moment is the time when you can be the best you. You can't be the best you tomorrow, right now. You can't be the best you a year ago, today. Of course, if you had a time machine, you could do some interesting things with the past and the future. (If you have a time machine, please send us a photo on Snapchat.) While that may, on the surface, seem like an easy thing ("be the best me I can be right now"), it's not. So much of your day functions as a distraction to you being your best self. It's hard to be your best self when you are stressed about a math exam that you have today. It's a challenge to be your World's Greatest Me when someone cuts in front of you in line. It's not easy to do one step better than yesterday when there is so much demanding your time today. It's almost like you get out of bed and are immediately moving from place to place without any time to sit and consider what today could hold. Moreover, throughout the day, because of the busyness of moving from task to task, it does not feel like there is any space to slow down and focus on what's happening and on how you could give your personal best in each individual moment. What's so sad about this is that this moment, this very second that you are reading these words, is the best time to be the greatest you. Right now is when you get to do something. Right now is when change is possible. How can you slow down and recognize moments where you are today and what you can do to make yourself better than yesterday?

Often, as a daily exercise, we suggest that you take a few moments at the start of your day to visualize your life and think about how you want to show up as "me" today. Visualization is a very powerful tool. Our minds are constructed in part to think in terms of sensory images. Right now, close your eyes and go to your kitchen. Are you in your kitchen? Walk to the refrigerator. Feel your hand on the door. What is the texture and temperature of the surface? Open the door. Feel the air hitting your skin. Reach inside your refrigerator to the top shelf. There, pick up a big, bright yellow lemon. Pull the lemon out of the fridge and hold it in one of your hands. What is the weight of the lemon? What is its temperature? What about the texture? Take the lemon over to one of the countertops nearby and cut the lemon in half. Now, take half the lemon up to your nose and inhale. What does the lemon smell like? Take another deep breath of that lemon smell. Now, put the lemon half between your lips and bite. Feel the sensation of biting into that lemon. What does it taste like? Hold it there for a moment. Now, open your eyes. Was there an increased amount of saliva in your mouth during this experience? Did your face squint or lips pucker up? Did you taste that lemon? Look around the room right now. There's probably not a real lemon anywhere to be found nearby. Because your mind is that powerful, you were able to experience a lemon even when it was not in the room. Any time you wanted today, you could go back to that lemon. As a leadership tool, this brand of visualization is exceedingly useful. You can visualize how you want to show up as your personal best in your world today.

Right now, you could do a similar visualization about being your World's Greatest Me. Close your eyes. Think about standing, sitting, or moving in your favorite place on campus:

Where are you right now?

What are you doing?

Who is around you?

What are they doing?

What does your body feel like right now?

What do you smell?

Do you taste anything?

What do you hear around you?

Now, think about you, as a whole person, in this place that you selected and are in right now:

Who are you?

Where have you come from?

Where are you today?

Where are you going?

Today, what is one way in which you want to show up one step better than you did yesterday?

What does it look like for you to do this?

What does it feel like to do this?

What do other senses (taste, smell, sound) register as you do this?

Now, come back to this room. Take a moment to record what you experienced in your leadership or personal journal.

This experience of pausing and considering how you could potentially approach your day today can be a profound step toward you becoming your World's Greatest Me each day. While your day may often start with the rush to get to school, the act of taking a few moments to pause and consider these questions can completely set the tone and intention of today. Also, this exercise, especially when done every single day, can offer you many clues about who you are, what you believe, and how you operate. You can look at what you visualize and ask many questions. Do you believe there's hope for today and the future? Do you want to be more than "okay" and functioning through your day? To what level of greatness do you wish to aspire today? During your third class today? During the first moments of your day? Right now?

As a student leader, this can provide further clues as to who you are, what you are doing, and how you are operating within your leadership team. Do you simply want to get the planning done for the homecoming (or whatever event you are working on today) so you can move on to the next event on your calendar? Are you focusing your energy as a leader on those who are easiest to provide your focus? Are you interested in only helping people when it's easy? Are you only celebrating a select few individuals on your campus? How are you treating your fellow group members? And, most important of all these questions, what are you going to do about this? While so many students today will go about their day with little idea of who they are, what they do, and how they operate, you can't operate as a student leader at that low-functioning level. The lives and futures of your fellow students are in your hands. Of course, your own life and future is in your hands too. So, what are you going to do about it? What are you going to do to explore your greatness, your personal best, today? What are you going to do to create significant moments for other people so they can explore their greatness today? You are that important. You're that important for yourself. You're that important to other people.

You can't do it alone. Others need to help you be your best. You need others to help you help others be their best. If you think back to our discussion about gifts, talents, and skills, we made it clear that you have a unique area of expertise that other students do not have. You have unique experiences that help make up who you are. You have unique offerings to provide yourself and the group. Likewise, others have unique gifts too, often ones that complement those areas of need that you have. Where you have a weakness, others may have a strength to help you with that. So, part of your job as a student leader is to develop and explore your greatness, your World's Greatest Me, so you can see where you are most able to help. It's like a group of people getting together to learn how to use their unique superpowers. Some are fire experts. Some are ice experts. Some are water experts. Individually, they have unique powers and one-of-a-kind weaknesses. However, together, they can help one another so that they are the strongest that they can be. What is your superpower when you are living as your personal best?

World's Greatest We

As a team of student leaders, one of your many roles is to support the individuals in your class in becoming their World's Greatest Me. If you were to undertake martial arts, what you'd notice about such a way of study is that errors are not hugely emphasized by one's peers. You'll often do ten thousand kicks or more without hearing anyone laugh or mock you for your attempts. In the martial arts environment, everyone is learning. There is a mutual respect for the fact that each person is at a different level of skill, working on different types of techniques. Not everyone will become a black belt, but each person is working on learning part of the overall form of becoming the best physical and mental being possible. Your leadership class should be that type of place, where there is such a great regard for the act of another person trying to do better at anything. When someone makes an attempt and fails, that's perfect – that's what working and trying to do well is all about: taking first steps, failing, getting back up, and trying again and again.

In your own first steps as a human being, you fell down. You did. However, there was someone there to help you. There was someone there to acknowledge you for the attempt. There was someone there who cared about you and maybe even provided you with some sort of support in how to do better next time. Someone was there to pick you up when you failed. There was someone there to celebrate you when you finally were able to walk on your own. Because of the environment of support that was present during your first steps, you were able to learn how to walk. Likewise, you want to create that exact type of safe place inside your leadership team so that people are encouraged to try, supported when they fail, and applauded when they finally succeed.

Your World's Greatest Me probably involves being the best support that you can be for others on your team. By adopting this first-step mentality regarding your team members, you are more able to be with them, help them, and celebrate them as they take steps. Be open and honest with yourself about your abilities and your disabilities. Where are you able to provide the most help to others? What are some areas of weakness where you are going to need the support of others? We all have areas in which we excel, and we all have areas where we struggle. You have to identify those gifts and needs, decide how you will challenge yourself today, and decide how you will help others as your personal best today. This is not a "random act of kindness" way of thinking, where you do something good when it's convenient for you to do so. Instead, this is about an overall way of thinking: "When I am being my best me, I have many gifts, talents, and skills that I can perfect and give to others. I also have areas of challenge in my life where I'm going to need others to use their gifts to help. As an individual I am powerful, but as a team we are the most powerful." Rather than taking up occasional good deeds, you should consider how you can be your personal best right now and how your team can come together to help each other do the same.

As a team, you need to constantly return, again and again, to who you are, what you do, and how you operate. You need to constantly be conversing about these topics so you don't fall into the trap of simply being a team that is here to do posters and prom. No one rolls out of bed and says, "I'm going to be as lousy as I possibly can today." So, we know that you and your team want to be about more than hanging signs on campus and throwing dances. Accordingly, there are a number of questions that you and your team should consider often:

What do we do as a team?

What actions will our team take each day to support each team member in being his or her World's Greatest Me?

How is each person significant and needed in these efforts? Am I significant? Is the person sitting next to me in my class needed? Why?

How am I vital to the success of this student leadership team?

What does each person in this class, including myself, have to offer one another?

What will we do as a team when someone is not providing his or her personal best for the team?

How is the team running the process of being our personal best together? Are we relying too much upon the teacher to set the agenda, keep the class running, and maintain productive order?

How are we waiting for the teacher, assistant principal, or principal to provide us with a vision, focus, tasks, etc., instead of taking it upon ourselves to operate at a high level, helping as many people as we possibly can in exploring their personal best?

To what degree do we have a Royal Family within this classroom? How do we exclude some students from positions of power? How do we show preference for some?

How are we helping the Kileys and Alyssas in this classroom?

How are we drawing out the Camo Kids?

How are we allowing our Austins to be the best Austins that they can be?

Considering first-step mentality, you and your team are going to fail. You are going to fall down. You are not going to live up to your goals and your beliefs. However, it does not have to stop there, like it does in many student leadership teams throughout the world. You don't have to settle. Instead, you can engage in conversations about the questions above, knowing that things are not perfect but that you can make them one step better than the day before. Just as people can look at themselves and strive to be their personal best today, your team can similarly envision what it would be like to be "our personal best" today. At the end of every day, you can ask, "How did we live up to our goals and beliefs?" At the start of each day with your team, you may ask, "How are we going to be our personal best together today?" The question is not, "Are we going to fail?" You will. The most appropriate question is what are you going to do about your failure? Will you ignore it? Will you mock your team's attempt? Will you punish, demean, and put down failings? Will you applaud an attempt made by your team? Will you celebrate, truly celebrate, when a success is experienced by your team when you lived up to your goals and beliefs?

Often, when we work with student leadership teams, we hear objections to the team doing the exceedingly hard work of being their personal best, because "the school does not have school spirit," "no one shows up," "people don't participate," or "they don't treat us like we deserve." First, the point of you working as the best team you can be has nothing to do with the recognition that others provide you for your work. *You* are not the point. The whole aim of your work as student leaders is to provide significant moments to others, where they can be their World's Greatest Me, and to put a spotlight on those moments of greatness. As student leaders, you are to constantly elevate others above yourselves without fail. Second, how can you expect others to believe in your team and buy in to what you are doing together when you are not operating as the best team you can be? Imagine the most despicable person you know giving you a dollar to buy a drink from the vending machine. While you may be grateful for the dollar, it's from this horrible person, which makes you unable to be fully thankful – you are quite suspicious of this person. Similarly, imagine getting an invitation to a party from a person so horrible that he or she might as well be a vampire. You would love to go to the party, but this blood-sucking person is running it, so you don't want to get involved. What if you and your leadership team are seen as being as bad as that vampire? If you knew nothing about this leadership team besides what it did and did not do on campus, would you want to participate? What, then, do you suppose is holding others back from being part of your efforts and being as excited to take part as you are? Perhaps you're not excited at all, and that may be the problem. If you're not passionate about this leadership thing, why would anyone want to be involved? If you were a restaurant and no one was coming through your doors, a smart business person would assume that something was wrong with the food or the customer service. If no one is participating with you, it's your problem. What are you going to do about it?

Only as your team works to be its best can you truly help the rest of the people at your school be their best.

The World's Greatest High School

As student leaders, you are to help every person on your campus become their personal best each day. By taking steps daily to be your own World's Greatest Me and by coming together as a team that is working to be the best "we" you can be, you are in a position as a leadership team where you can begin making some amazing new moves on behalf of others. Like we mentioned in one of the previous chapters, when you are not sure about how or if to proceed as a student leader, it's often good practice to try something you have never tried before.

When you and your team members are ready to take some bold new actions as a team on behalf of the students at your school, there are a number of questions you can ask yourselves to provide clues about what you should do next. As we discuss each of these questions, think about the people you serve. Think about the Austins, the Kileys and Alyssas, the Camo Kids, the Royal Family, and others. Consider discussing these questions as a whole class and seeing what ideas you and your team can come up with. You'll be quite surprised with what will emerge.

First, do you have someone who encourages you to explore your greatness? Do you have a teacher who encourages you? Do you have a fellow student who supports you in this way? Do you have a friend who truly understands you, your needs, and how he or she can help? As you think about all the students who are on your campus each day, how would they answer these questions? You'll see that there are many areas of opportunity. There are students on your campus who will not have their name said a single time by anyone the entire day. There are students who walk your halls without ever making eye contact with anyone. Some students may believe that no one would notice if they were not there (except their teachers, who would punish them for not being in class). You have students who feel relatively alone in pursuing their dreams. Many students don't even share their dreams and aspirations. Accordingly, how will your student leadership team be a source of encouragement to others? How will you work to put teachers or mentors together with each and every student? How can you and your team see what needs exist in your peers and fulfill those needs? How will you and your team ensure that there is no one on campus who can simply disappear? Consider these questions as a team.

Second, do you have situations in which you are permitted to be your World's Greatest Me? How does your leadership team manufacture moments where other students can explore their greatness? As leaders, moments like these are where you get to see others grow. You're able to see what gifts, talents, and skills are present in individuals. You get to see their needs too. You get a picture of what brand of support these people will need going forward. How do you create opportunities for others to try, fail, and succeed? How do you help others recognize how they did and take next steps to do better next time? How do you help others grow? How do you purposely, actively attempt to change the lives and impact the futures of the unrecognized students of your school? Right now, students may not have anyone actively coaching them or creating opportunities for them to shine. How do you create spotlights on greatness? How many "players" do not have a field or stage on which they can shine? How do you create the platforms on which others can be seen and celebrated? How do you find the unknown students? To what degree do you behave as if people would be worse off without you? Would others be worse off if you did not exist as a team? Think about a school where your leadership team did not exist. Would just the flyers, posters, and dances be missed? What do you do to help other people grow every single day?

Third, who gets the credit when something amazing happens at one of your events, rallies, celebrations, etc.? Do you get the credit? Do the others outside of your student leadership team get most of the spotlight? Do they get most of the credit? How do you celebrate more than athletic greatness? What percentage of your events spotlight athletic greatness over other types of greatness? What types of greatness besides sports do you showcase throughout the year? How do you celebrate the Kileys and Alyssas? How do you draw out the Camo Kids? Are your celebrations the end of the story for those whom you put in the spotlight? How do you and your leadership team further support those who were celebrated on an ongoing basis throughout the year and beyond? Whose greatness do you acknowledge and celebrate?

Your actions define who you are, what you believe, and what you value. You can't demand that other people be part of your vision. Ten people in a room cannot decide the vision of the school, put up a bunch of posters with the vision, and expect others to live it out each day. Likewise, you can't demand that others at your school fully believe you and trust you with their safety and personal well-being from the start. There will be many people who will be skeptical of you – they have been hurt many times before. So, you and your team members have to constantly work with one another to keep this work going consistently throughout the year. So many student leadership teams get so busy preparing for the fall and spring rallies, throwing prom, and getting ready for graduation. What about all that time in between? Does the presence of your student leadership team disappear for weeks or months on end? Does your student leadership team wind down or disappear after homecoming? It's through the regular work of your team and its members that you are able to convince others that you are truly interested in supporting them in becoming their personal best. You can't fake that. You can't wear a t-shirt that has some clichéd leadership saying on it and act like you don't care about other human beings. You can't call yourself a student leader if you treat others like they are less deserving than you. Further, you can't call yourself a leader if you have little or no interest in seriously working harder than you ever have before to become your World's Greatest Me so that you can be part of the World's Greatest Student Leadership Team and can build the World's Greatest High School. Your work as a student leader and as a member of a student leadership team will sometimes be a matter of life and death. So, what are you going to do?

Who are you?

What do you do?

How do you operate?

There will come a time at some point in the future when someone is going to need you. This person is going to need you just about as much as he or she needs to breathe. Will you be there for that person? Will you be ready to help him or her?

Are you comfortable in your own skin, or are you

trying to be someone you are not? Stop trying to be someone you are not! Our hope is that you recognize that it's up to you to work each day to be your best self so that you can help others as your World's Greatest Me. While you will most definitely benefit from being your personal best, others are counting on you to show up with your gifts, talents, and skills in full force. Your team cannot be the World's Greatest Student Leaders without you bringing your best. They can't help others as much as they possibly can unless you bring the ultimate you through that classroom door. Likewise, every student on campus is counting on you and your team. They will not be the same without you. You are that needed. Today is your best chance to be the World's Greatest Me that has ever shown up in the world. Will you answer the call to be this for yourself so that you can help others do the same? If not, it's time to transfer to another class.

BLUEPRINT QUESTIONS:

----

1. What needs your attention most today? Why?

2. Who needs your attention most today? Why?

3. Describe a person, real or imaginary, who understands you and your needs. What is the best way such a person could help you with one specific need you have in your life?

4. Describe a situation, real or imaginary, where you are permitted to use and stretch a gift, talent, or skill you care for greatly. How could

the student leadership team create a situation where you were able to do this? What would that look like?

5. When you and your student leadership team are engaging in events on campus, who gets the credit for the amazing things that happen at these rallies or celebrations? Do you get the credit? Does your team get the credit? How could you ensure that the spotlight is on the greatness of others outside your team?

DARES:

---

1. On your own, undertake the breathing exercise described earlier in this chapter.

2. On your own, undertake the visualization exercise described earlier in this chapter. Write out your experience in your journal.

3. As a student leadership team, discuss and process the questions from the "World's Greatest We" section of this chapter.

4. As a student leadership team, discuss and process the Blueprint Questions above.

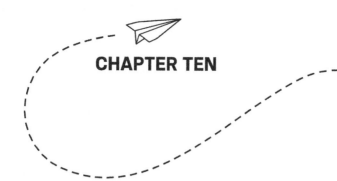

CHAPTER TEN

EVERYTHING WE DO, WE DO WITH PRIDE

"Quite often, what student leaders and their teams believe about who they are, what they do, and how they operate does not match up with their actions at large."

Graduation Day. The arena was filled with thousands of excited parents and family members of the graduates of Chris's class. Mothers and fathers were standing in their chairs, pointing their arms and saying, "There is my baby! That's my baby!" as many proud and some embarrassed teenagers smiled with anticipation. This was it. After over a dozen years and tens of thousands of hours of work, the graduating class was finally in their seats ready to walk across the stage and finish with a diploma in their hands. These students admired their caps and gowns. As they sat in their chairs, a silence came over the crowd. The ceremony was starting. Through numerous speakers, more and more students began to look around at one another while listening to the men and women speaking on the stage. Of all these people whom they had seen for so long each day, they probably would only see a few ever again. Some began to think about the memories of those years together. Some were ecstatic, others were solemn, and many were tearful. This chapter of life was finally coming to a close, and a new one was beginning. Finally, the music began, and the first row of students stood and took their place to climb up, walk across the stage, and get their diplomas. As each was handed his or her diploma, the student basked in his or her four seconds of fame, his or her moment in the spotlight of greatness, thinking, "YES! I did it!" One row went, and another, and another. Students began to see the rows getting closer and closer to them until it was their turn to take the stage. Many thought something like, "This is it; this is my time." It was finally Chris's time to walk across that stage. In his wheelchair, Chris could feel his heart pumping in his chest. It was his time. His younger, sophomore sister came forward with the walker that they had arranged to use for this special event. Looking into his eyes, she placed it in front of him as he readied his body. He took a deep breath and tensed his muscles. He stood. With his sister holding the walker steady, Chris walked forward one step after another after another. Finally, he shook the hand of the master of ceremonies and received his diploma. Emotion overtook the attendees. His fellow students stood, giving a standing ovation, followed by the parents, family members, and other guests. The crowd and Chris both celebrated this significant moment together. He had finally walked across that stage and graduated.

Each day leading to that stage, Chris lived as his personal best in pursuit of his goals, values, and beliefs as a way of life. Are the goals, values, and beliefs of your school or leadership team your way of life? If not, why not? On one level, it's possible that you might not be able to even name what the goals, values, and beliefs of your school or leadership team are! If you're at the end of this book, reading this chapter, we're quite curious about what conditions could exist within your school or leadership team to allow this to be the case. On another level, it's possible that your stated goals, values, and beliefs as a team are simply artwork on the wall – that is, these are not part of the daily actions and way of thinking for you as a person, team member, and student of your school at large. Think about that: It's possible that you, your leadership team, and your school community as a whole are meeting each day, have mission statements, student learning outcomes, goals, values, and beliefs on posters, letterheads, brochures, and websites in and around the school, and are not living those out as if they were the guiding principles of who you are, what you do, and how you operate. These all tell your story. Everyone on campus will know if your story is real or not. What is the value of big ideas when no one is learning, considering, and living them? All those posters, slogans, and false words just become artwork on the wall. Live a way of life; don't just talk about a way of life. Your culture must be lived, not just talked about.

In this book, we have presented to you a way of life. It's not a complete way of life, but it's a great start. It's up to you to personally consider what has been presented here and make a decision about how you apply this to your own personal journey. As a team, you'll have to do the same. You'll have to consider if this book is simply something assigned by your teacher or if this book can provide clues to how your team can grow to help more and more individuals become their World's Greatest Me each day. Your fellow student leaders, with your help, will have to consider what aspects of this way of living are worth their time. As a whole school, you'll have to contend with the disruption that the ideas mentioned in this book could cause if you enacted them. After all, there is a Royal Family that has enjoyed the focus for much time. Perhaps there are members of the Royal Family within your classroom who don't want to let go of the power and the spotlight. There are educators who are used to certain activities and traditions at your school. You'll have to help them understand why things are changing and where things are going and invite them in to shift to your school's new way of living out its goals, beliefs, and values.

Think about what would happen to your school community if nearly everyone was engaged and living out the values of the World's Greatest High School. What if everyone felt they worked at or attended the World's Greatest school? It's not "the best school in the world," it's "our greatest school that we can be." What would your school look like? What would it be like to do everything suggested in this volume? As an individual, this would be, potentially, the journey of a lifetime toward your World's Greatest Me. As a team, you could come together and become exceedingly stronger than if you kept business as usual. As a school, you could, stated quite plainly, change the lives and impact the futures of thousands and thousands of individuals for this generation and generations to come. We're not exaggerating here.

The sixth value of the World's Greatest High School is, "Everything we do, we do with PRIDE." This value means that the people who make up the World's Greatest High School live out their goals, beliefs, and values every day. It means that the actions taken by you, your team, and your school community as a whole match up with your words. If you have posters all over campus that say, "We believe all students have futures," then every person in your school is taking actions each day that show that value is true here. If you say that "no one gets anywhere without a teacher," then your school clearly treats teachers as the revered members of the community that the value implies. Essentially, "everything we do, we do with PRIDE" means that you are "walking your talk" – that is, your actions and your words are the same thing.

Walking Your Talk

Are you a work of fact or fiction? Quite often, what

student leaders and their teams believe about who they are, what they do, and how they operate does not match up with their actions at large. While so many students will put on t-shirts that designate them as student leaders, attend leadership conferences, and happily list their participation in leadership on their college applications, their actions do not match up with what they claim they stand for. The journey that we have described in this book is about a way of life and a belief system. It's not about a way of posters. It's not about a way of t-shirt slogans. It's not about lip-service to ideals that you do not live out on a daily basis. It's a journey – a way of life. Who you are, what you do, and how you operate is displayed by your interactions with others. Your values are clear for the whole world to see based upon how you conduct yourself as a human being at your school and beyond. Your beliefs are clearly displayed by what you do as well. What you create as a person, team, and school communicates much more about you than your words. What people see you doing each day is what people come to know as you. So, if you are a work of fact, your actions will match up with what you claim to stand for. If you are a work of fiction, it will be entirely clear to much of the world that you are a fake. You can't fake leadership. Your actions matter. Your actions will define you as a leader, a dictator, a slacker, or a faker. Your actions will define your class as true "student leadership" or as the "posters and prom class." The choice is yours. This choice will be made every day. Your decision will be marked by your action. Show your choice to your peers every day.

The choice is yours. Over the course of this book, at length, we've discussed your possible path to greatness. Just like the paper airplane on the cover of this text, not one of us will take the same route as another to reach our destinations. You are going to make a set of personal choices each day that determine the path to greatness that you take. You get to choose if you live in no hope, in mediocrity, or along a path toward your World's Greatest Me. You get to decide how you are going to show up for yourself, for your team, and for others in your school community. The actions that you take each day cannot be determined by your team, by your teachers, by your administrators, or by the words and slogans that adorn the walls of your school. It all starts with you and your personal choices in each singular moment of each day. It starts with your decision to move toward your personal best, to stand still, or to resign without hope.

Your student leadership team and your fellow students on campus need you to do the daily work of walking your path to greatness. They don't need inauthentic words. They don't need silly, impersonal gifts. They don't need posters. **They need you**. They need you to serve. When you have made the choice to be the best you each day in each moment, you are most able to serve. You become more aware of who you are. You begin to understand that you have to contribute. You can recognize your own gifts and talents. You can perfect your skills. From this standpoint, you, then, have something to contribute. You can contribute to your own success. You can give toward the success of your student leadership team. You can work with them to usher in, cultivate, and celebrate the developing gifts, talents, and skills of others. Everyone benefits. However, it starts with you.

You, personally – you, as an individual, are that important! You could say, "If I can be my personal best, we can be our greatest, so we can help others become their World's Greatest Me." Imagine if everyone on your student leadership team gave their personal best every day, at every event, and with every meeting with fellow human beings. What would your team accomplish? No matter what you will do with your team or what you will do as a whole school, none of that can happen ultimately unless you walk your talk and work each day to be your World's Greatest Me. As you are about to go out on your own, with your team, and alongside your school community to change the lives and impact the futures of students at your school, we want to provide you with a picture, via the suggestions that follow, of what it would look like to "go all in" toward becoming the World's Greatest High School – as if everything you were doing as an individual, as a team, and as a school was at the peak of possibility. For each area of work, we'll make some suggestions about what you can do, what your team can do, and what your school as a whole can do to help each person work each day to become his or her World's Greatest Me. This chapter is about showing you what it would look like to truly walk your talk.

Create a Culture of Significance

Begin with yourself. Next, advance your team and others.

Me

If you believe that everyone matters, your actions will show this belief. You can't "do" leadership. Leadership springs from within you – that is, leadership emanates from the core of you as a person. Does your personal leadership shout from the hilltops, "You matter!" or does it show that you see people in terms of winners and losers, insiders and outsiders, part of the Royal Family and others? When it's just you working by yourself or interacting with one or two other people, what do your actions say? Do they say that you see everything that you do as a potential significant step toward your future? Do your actions say that you think that the people with whom you interact are significant? To what extent do your actions clearly communicate that you are worth your own time? What you do in every moment will either build a case that you are who you say you are or will prove that you are dishonest about your ideals. Don't wear a leadership t-shirt unless you are willing to be put to the daily test of thousands of eyes. Are you who you say you are?

If you want to create a culture of significance at your school, you first have to believe that each person is needed, wanted, and valued and important. From there, with that knowledge firmly in place, you can do so much: Greet others. Introduce yourself. Have ongoing conversations with people you don't know. Let your actions communicate that others matter and that someone cares about them. Let your behavior show that you are someone who recognizes the gifts and talents of others and tells them that you are there to help them be the best that they can be.

We

Collectively, as a student leadership class, have you set aside time to get to know one another? We have a human need in groups to be recognized for our talents. Do you provide chances for you and your fellow classmates to explore your greatness with one another, in the safety of this class? Do you provide ways in which people can name, demonstrate, and develop their skills? Do you create a place where you and your classmates feel that you get to do what you do best? How many times do you take a "time out" to discuss what's happening and not happening regarding your teammates? How do you take time to reveal what's going on in the individual lives of your team members? Is there space for you and your leadership team to understand the life burdens that are influencing the work of your peers? We have observed many times when student leaders are oblivious to the hardships experienced by their classmates – that is, hardships involving people close to them, debilitating negative thoughts, and feelings of hopelessness. No positive can come from such no-hope situations. Would you be aware of such situations if they emerged within your group? How can you say that you believe in creating a culture of significance where everyone matters if you are not even aware of the difficulties being experienced by members of your own small group?

Creating such a culture in your own classroom has to start with the heart of each person within the class. Each person must believe that everyone matters. From there, your class can work together to focus upon the gifts of each member. Your teammates can work to recognize the unique significance of everyone. Think back to your last event, rally, or celebration. Was there a group of people within your team who had more important roles than others? Did some receive more focus than others? Did you celebrate and acknowledge the contribution of each person, or did you tend to focus upon recognizing one group within your class? Consider the ways in which your class can explore how each of its members matters and provide opportunities for each member to shine and put him or her in the spotlight.

Others
Quite similarly to working to emphasize the importance of each person within your classroom, you have to create that same level of significance for everyone outside as well. If you say you believe that all kids have futures and that everyone is gifted and talented, could you look and see evidence of that in the ways that you work with people outside your classroom? Do your campaigns and rallies truly focus on the contributions of all? Alternatively, do your rallies function simply as a fancy way of celebrating the same people (often the Royal Family) over and over again? Do you seek out the contributions of and attempt to make significant daily moments for Camo Kids, Kileys and Alyssas, and Austins? If your answer is not an easy "yes," with some

clear examples of how you do that, then much work has to be done.

Challenge yourself to find ways to celebrate individual greatness. Take the blinders off and walk your campus, and start making a list of the great things that are taking place day in and day out. Then, celebrate, acknowledge, and let people know that they matter.

A Culture of First-Step Mentality

Ninety-nine out of one hundred leadership students believe what they do as a team is meant to build up people rather than tear them down. However, when you look into the details of how many student leadership teams operate, they don't necessarily build up their individual members, themselves, or people outside their classrooms. The reason for this is simple: It's easier to emphasize and own abilities over disabilities. It's easier for someone to say, "I'm really great at speaking in front of groups!" and much less easy to say, "I need to work on how I treat other team members during stressful situations." As individuals, team members, and members of the whole school, it's your duty to own your weaknesses and develop them.

Me

As an individual student leader, the best thing that you can do is be aware of your own failures. Be aware of those areas in which you need to grow. Looking at our challenges is not something we should be afraid of; it should be part of the learning experience. There's nothing we've done that we've done like the best ever on the first try. So, the first time you step into a leadership position, the first time you're asked to be the head of a committee, or the first time you are going to paint a poster, don't be scared to be in a place where failure is possible. If you're a freshman or new to the leadership team, you may have a fear of painting posters and meeting the expectations of the class, so you may choose not to paint that poster and not want to put yourself in a situation where you may expose your weaknesses. You have to overcome that. If you believe that you are working to be a better "me" today than yesterday, you have to be willing to fail and build on the shortcomings of yesterday.

Your willingness to fail is such an important concept. You need to put your gifts, talents, and skills into action today and enjoy the experience. Take the first step. Understand that mastery does not occur at your first step. However, what you do today could be *your* World's Greatest. It could be the world's greatest attempt because you will give your personal best. As an individual, dare to give yourself permission to fail so you can grow to be your personal best.

We

As a leadership team, acknowledge the gifts, talents, and skills of everyone on your team. Provide opportunities for others to dare to be brave because you have their back. It's like when a senior reaches out to a freshman student and says, "Hey, I've been noticing how hard you are working, and I think you would be great to try out this other leadership task." When members of the class take on the first-step mentality that says, "We believe this is the best place in which our teammates can be their personal best, even if they fail; failure is a part of the learning process, like learning to walk or learning to ride a bike," team members can encourage one another, and they can provide the safe space in which someone can make a first attempt at anything. It's in situations like these that you and your team members feel the most free to be stretched and grow, because there is the chance to do something new and the safety to try and fail.

Others

To help your entire school, you have to slowly create a cultural environment where first steps are welcomed, supported, and celebrated. This is the type of culture wherein one could easily say, "I know that as a member of this class or group, I'm expected to stretch myself; I'm expected to step up; I'm expected to go to the next level, whatever that might be. I know that I'll be supported when I make new moves and even when I fail; therefore, I know it's safe to try." If it is not understood that failure is part of learning and exploring one's greatness, then that is a "No Hope" situation. In such a culture, where failure is feared or avoided, your exploration of your greatness will be hindered or will cease entirely. Create a culture where exploration of greatness is encouraged and expected. Create a culture where the celebration of the journey is far more important than the celebration of a destination. Create a school where strong attempts are recognized more than mediocre finishes.

Create a Common Language

Stop leadership class right now. Ask every single student to silently write down the goal of the leadership class, along with your leadership team's beliefs and values. Have one person collect them all. Have the instructor read them all word-for-word. Chances are, what you will have are twenty-five or so different responses to the same question. For you to be truly successful as a student leadership team, you need to have a common language, where everyone understands who you are, what you do, and how you operate. Unless you know and can speak in this common language, how can you live out these values as a way of life as a team?

Me

As an individual student, you have to ask yourself what you believe about the World's Greatest Values discussed in this book. Do you agree with these? Can you operate in your daily work as a student leadership team member supporting these values? What additional values do you have as an individual that you bring into the leadership team? If you cannot agree with one of the values that the class states that it stands for, you have to be brave enough to stand up and say, "I don't agree with that!" More importantly, by knowing your own values, you may have to be brave enough to stand up to the rest of your leadership team members when they are not living up to the values they say they stand for. One day, you may have to say, "We say we want to create a culture of significance for all, but we are failing this certain group on campus." What are your values? Do you agree with the values of your leadership team?

We

As a leadership team, you need to post your goals, beliefs, and values on the wall of your classroom. Your team needs to go to staff meetings and regularly say, "Hi, we're the leadership class. One of our goals this year is to 'create a culture of significance on this campus where everyone matters.' So, we wanted to tell you about how you can support us students the best you can this month." Your team needs to have representation at administrative meetings with regular sit-downs with your principal, assistant principal, activities director or leadership teacher, and other major teachers on campus, where you communicate who you are as a leadership team, what you do, and how you operate. You need to be aware of the importance of connecting and engaging students in the power of relationship. Your team needs to regularly discuss its goals, beliefs, and values, as if they are the lifeblood of what you do each and every day rather than some poster on the wall that has little or no meaning because everyone is so busy creating balloon arches for the next event. Discover your goals, beliefs, and values; post them, discuss them, and constantly evaluate if you are living those out each day. These are crucial in creating a culture of significance at the World's Greatest High School, Middle School, or Elementary School.

Others

When working with the rest of the school, think about "public relations" in the sense that you, the leadership team, are a business. As a business, what does your work as a leadership team communicate? What is your product? What are your services? How do you treat and serve your customers? How is your customer service? Is your product or service for everyone? Or is it only for a small group of people? When your rally is over, what message or experience did other students take away? Did you and your team truly meet the goals, beliefs, and values that you claim that you stand for? Did they validate your actions?

Consider grabbing a handful of students after your next event. Choose people whom you do not know and interview them as a class. Ask them, "What do you think our goal was in throwing this event?" and "What did our actions communicate?" What do you think they will say? Ideally, what your participants experience will be a direct match to the goals, beliefs, and values of your class. If not, much work has to be done.

Opportunities to Be World's Greatest

When you are your personal best, you can help others do the same.

Me

How do you create opportunities for you to be the World's Greatest Me? One way is that you have to take on a greater role as a leader. Create opportunities to stretch yourself. Consider what you do in situations where others are calling upon you to do more, give more, step up, stretch, etc. Do you hold back in fear of failure? Do you not want to step out and expose yourself, expose your weaknesses, or expose your disabilities? Remember, everyone has weaknesses, disabilities, and insecurities. You have an opportunity to overcome your insecurities and take the first steps to be the best you today that has ever walked this earth. Each day, you have to renew your commitment to be your personal best. If you are not willing to do this, are you truly a student leader? Or, alternatively, are you simply a kid who's signed up for the leadership class to get some credits?

Each one of us has weaknesses, disabilities, and challenges. That's okay! However, these do not have to stop you from being your personal best. Maybe you're being encouraged to do something you've never done before. Maybe you've never had an opportunity to make a balloon arch, lead a committee, or speak in front of a large group at a rally. To become your personal best, you have to take on challenges that will stretch you. Look for mentors who can help you in these moments. Opportunities to be your personal best are everywhere, but you have to take them on. You have to do something today that you have never done before. Enjoy the ride of exploring your greatness! Where are you holding back? Why?

We

As a team, you can create opportunities for greatness in many ways. You can create the type of environment in your leadership class where the daily, individual contributions of team members are expected – that is, where not a day will go by without each student showing what he or she is doing for the good of the group's cause. You can take notice of the gifts, talents, and skills of each group member, seeing his or her individual, unique abilities. You can place students in situations where each gets to exercise and better his or her talents. You can allow people to fail. You can place a spotlight when someone shows the best to the world he or she ever has before in a certain skill.

Others

When working outside your classroom with the rest of the school, put in the spotlight others who perform acts of personal greatness. Find ways to acknowledge others in a way that you never have before. Think about situations in which greatness is currently displayed on your campus: Do you walk by without saying anything? Do you just pass by and say, "Oh, well, that's not a star athlete's performance," or "That's not a top-notch academic performance"? Expand your definition of who is deserving of recognition, as if the attempt and the journey toward greatness were most important. How about putting the spotlight on someone who displays kindness or compassion? What about putting the spotlight on someone during a time of need, where the acknowledgement that you give could be what saves and protects that person?

Explore Your Greatness

How can you and your team help others to explore their greatness?

Me

As a student leader, you are being asked to be on a continual quest to be the best you that the world has ever seen. Rather than leaving the day to chance, hoping that things will turn out for the best, you have taken up the call to intentionally make yourself your World's Greatest Me every day. To help you in this work, just like it's important for your leadership team to do, create a verbal picture of who you are, what you do, and how you operate. Create a personal greatness list where you list your strengths and abilities. Don't just list those things at which you are the best. Instead, list those things that you feel make you happy and more able to face your work. Create a needs list. What are those areas in yourself that you need to further develop to best assist yourself and others? Create a list of insecurities. What are those things about you that make you less comfortable in your own skin? What, inside yourself, prevents you from doing that which is required to take first steps and, potentially, fail? Understand that the you who is sitting reading this book right now cannot do better without trying and failing.

We

What can the leadership team do? Collectively, set up opportunities in the class to be able to share your abilities and your disabilities. Create a team culture in which someone may say, "I want to know the three things that you do well, because then I can match my disabilities to your abilities so that we can be a stronger team. Your weaknesses are my strengths. My strengths are your weaknesses. We're going to come together to help one another become the best we can be." When this type of communication emerges within the class, mentorship becomes more possible, because people know the areas in which you have expertise and the areas in which you need assistance. It's through this open discussion of your abilities and disabilities that your team members can best support one another so each person can be his or her personal best so the team can be its World's Greatest.

Others

What about when you work with others outside the leadership class? Think about the events that you host. What events can you create that acknowledge greatness? Look for ways to include the talents of others, outside your team, in what you are doing. Have you ever reached out to somebody who you saw doing some artistic work, asking them to do your posters and murals for your events? Look for people who you can include to make them part of your team. Squash the thinking that says, "Oh, no, we can't involve them; we're in charge of the rally!" If your job was to create the stage on which others could shine, would you not want to find people outside your team with great abilities so you could showcase them to the rest of the school? Take time to notice somebody. Acknowledge that person.

Invite him or her to be part of what you are doing. Provide this person with the chance to have his or her greatness seen by everyone else. Stand back and watch others be blessed by the work that you and your team have done. That's the point of your work as a student leader: to create the stages on which others can be seen and recognized for their emerging greatness. We challenge each of you to go find one person demonstrating greatness throughout campus and bring back an idea of how you could celebrate or acknowledge him or her. That's what you should be doing every day.

Our Actions Matter

The actions of you and your team could mean the world to another student.

Me

Pick any moment of your day so far. For example, consider the first five minutes that you walked onto campus. Did that moment accurately reflect who you are, what you do, and how you operate? If the whole world were going to build their ideas about you based upon these five minutes, would you say that these were the best five minutes for them to see? What would they have seen? What did your ways of walking communicate? Eye contact? Did you speak to anyone? Did you lean in? Alternatively, did you cross your arms and stay silent when around others? As a student leader, you are to endeavor to ask these types of questions about your actions and be aware of what you are doing. If you are not noticing, someone is. It's not that you want to put on a perfect image so you can stay on the leadership team and get another nice thing to say on your résumé. Instead, the point is that leaders are mindful of what they are doing, because what they do says much about who they are. So, today, think about the ways that you interact with other human beings. Consider how you talked mostly about you, about them, or did not talk at all. Reflect upon how you worked: Was it so you could be the best you, the same you, or just because it was required? Every moment provides a chance to show who you are. Every moment shows that, whether you want it to or not.

We

Likewise, look at what your group is doing each day. How does the rest of this campus see you? If you pulled random students aside at lunch and asked them on film, "What do you think about the leadership class?" what would they say? Does your team take daily steps to treat every person on campus as if they mattered? Does your team communicate that they are there to help everyone experience significance on campus? Do other students see your team as part of what's making the campus better, or are you part of what is making them feel more isolated, friendless, and alone? You may be surprised by what you hear. What if every complaint about your team was valid in some way? What would you do about it? Your team already has a reputation on campus. Chances are, it's accurate, at least in part. It's up to your team to show who you are, what you do, and how you operate.

Others

Accordingly, your actions with and around others matter. Do you acknowledge the World's Greatest Teachers? Do you celebrate the World's Greatest Custodians? Do something today that you never have done before. Identify one ability that someone outside your classroom has that is unique and of value. Celebrate that person. Create an "Explore Greatness" board in your classroom, and every day for an entire week, list what each of your group members has seen on campus that was greatness on display. The following week, assign groups and small teams to some of the people and groups that you listed. Help these people outside your team by inviting them to be part of an event you are throwing the following week. Create a greatness showcase on your campus, where each event puts on display the best of what each person (all persons) on campus has to offer. Include the Camo Kids, the Kileys and Alyssas, and the Austins.

What If?

What would your school become if everyone knew they were significant? What if everyone was applauded for their significance? What if everyone had an opportunity for a Rose Petal Moment? What if everyone left their graduation ceremony with no regrets? What if everyone truly matters? What if?

What would happen to the culture of your school if you took the actions described in this chapter each day? It would be absolutely amazing. It would be the type of place that allowed people to wake up each morning knowing that they were attending the ultimate place that could support them in becoming their personal best. What would you feel about such a place? Would you be interested in attending such a school? Are you willing to put in the time that it will take to build such a place? When you're building your World's Greatest School, whether it's a middle school, a high school, or an elementary school, it's not just about a place but a way of life as well. Are you willing to take up the way of life described here? The choice is yours.

BLUEPRINT QUESTIONS:

1. In what ways does your student leadership team walk their talk? Where does the student leadership team not do what they say they believe or stand for?

2. In what ways can you create a culture of significance? Provide examples.

3. In what ways can you foster a first-step mentality at your school?

4. What are the goals, beliefs, and values of your student leadership team?

DARES:

1. Ask the entire student leadership team to silently write down the goals of the leadership class, along with your student leadership team's beliefs and values. Have one person collect

them all. Have the instructor read them all word-for-word. Discuss the similarities and differences. Discuss: "Did we all write the same thing? What does that mean?"

2. Create a roster of the names of your student leadership team members. For each person, list a unique skill or talent that he or she has related to the work of your team. Poster creator? Balloon arch trainer? Announcer? Organizer? Remember, all students are gifted and talented. Show that.

3. Create an "Explore Greatness" board in your classroom. Every day for the entire week, list what each of your team members has seen on campus that was "greatness on display." The following week, assign small teams to some of the people and groups listed on your board. Invite these individuals to help your student leadership team in creating an event or being part of an event the next week.

4. As a whole class, list the Rose Petal Moments created by individual members of the team and by the team as a whole.

   a. Who was acknowledged during these Rose Petal Moments?

   b. What were they acknowledged for?

5. Discuss for whom your team could create moments in the spotlight. Who has never been spotlighted in the recent history of your school?

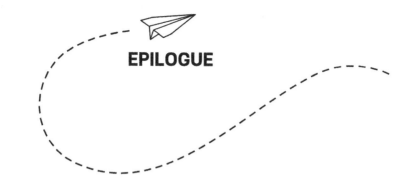

LEAVING WITH NO REGRETS

"I am able to stand before you today and tell you that the decisions you make now will affect the rest of your life."

This is the actual text of Chris's speech to his graduating class in the spring of 1999:

"How many of you remember what you were doing on May 30th of last year? I do. On that day, I dove into a lake and broke my neck. That one moment changed my life forever. From that day forward, I have had to fight. First, I fought for my life, and since then, I have fought just to be able to move. Everything is difficult, twenty-four hours a day. But the struggle I've gone through is worth it. The doctors all said that I would never move again, maybe not even feed myself. But I'm able to stand here before you today because of a lot of hard work. And

whether you realize it or not, all of you helped me get here.

You're probably wondering why I'm telling you all of this. Well, what I have gone through the past eight months is much like what all of us have been going through all of our lives; it's just on a different level. Each day is a new challenge. What if you had given up when you were first learning to ride a bike? How many times did you fall first? Or how about learning to swim? We all swallowed a little chlorine before we learned to stay afloat. And don't we all put in a huge amount of effort to be part of the crowd, to have friends? We have learned that over the years, we have to do certain things or behave a certain way to get the results we want. And how bad we want something has determined the effort we put into it.

Over the next four months, all of us here will be faced with another challenge: to do what has to be done to graduate. We have all spent pretty much our entire lives, as we remember them, going to school. For some, it has been easier than for others. But, you know what, we're all still here. For those of you who have had a more difficult time in school over the years, you have something to be especially proud of. You have stuck it out, even when the going was rough. That says something about you. There are some of you here today who are borderline as far as graduating. Don't give up now. You've made it through high school for three and a half years; there's only four months left. Look deep inside and decide what you're made of. Think about what you want your life to be like in the next fifty years. If you don't struggle through these next four months, you'll be struggling a lot more for many years to come. Without a diploma, there aren't too many jobs you can get that pay more than minimum wage. Is that what you really want?

For the past eight months, I have struggled. I have fought through something that I hope none of you have to ever go through. But my efforts are paying off. I am able to stand before you today and tell you that the decisions you make now will affect the rest of your life. You only get one chance at graduation. You get a few seconds in the spotlight, and then you will be done forever. What do you want those few seconds to be like?

On May 30th, 1998, I started a brand new life. On June 17th, 1999, I will be starting over again, as will you. The choices you make now will affect that new life. Do we want to begin our existence as independent adults with regrets or with memories that we can keep forever? I prefer good memories."

RICHARD PARKHOUSE

Park is an author and the founder of the "World's Greatest Schools" consultant team that is committed to creating a "culture of significance where everyone matters." They focus on "helping others explore their greatness." You can see the success of this process with his recognition system Spotlight On Greatness™. Park has had the opportunity to inspire greatness in over 2,000 schools and has assisted them in developing positive and interactive school climates. His work includes collaborating with schools to clearly communicate their beliefs, values, and purpose. Park believes all students are gifted and talented and every day they should be working to become the World's Greatest versions of themselves by always demonstrating their personal best!

Add Park on Snapchat

@parksgreatest
www.edalchemy.com

ABOUT THE AUTHORS

GUY E. WHITE, ED.D.

"Dr. Guy" is a Southern California teacher, professor, and highly sought-after international public speaker. He's the author of four books, including this one. Dr. Guy is a National Board Certified Teacher® by the National Board of Professional Teaching Standards and a

certified Integral Master Coach™ by Integral Coaching Canada: both "gold standard" accreditations in the teaching and coaching fields, respectively.

Integral Master Coach™ is a registered trademark in Canada owned by Integral Coaching Canada Inc. and licensed to Guy E. White.

National Board Certified Teacher® is a registered trademark of the National Board for Professional Teaching Standards and is used herein with permission.

Add Dr. Guy on Snapchat

@guyewhite
www.guyewhite.com

THANK YOU

BACKERS

Park and I send our sincerest, warmest thanks to the following people who believed in and backed our project – even before a single page was written.

LARRY & GINNY BIDDLE

MICHAEL ADAMS

BRYAN L. MURPHY * DOUGLAS E. JONES

THE NAVARRO'S * LARRY & RENEE GAINES

KRISTEN M. WHITE, PSY.D. * RYAN COMPARATO * ROB & BARBARA MADDEN * BRIAN COUSHAY * GRADY JENNINGS * JP & PAUL GILLIS * RICHARD J. NOBLETT * PETER BAUERFEIND * KELLI SANDUSKY * FRANCIE WARD * RON WARD * SARA COWEY CATALLI * MARK RODRIGUEZ * LANCE SHOEN * LINDA DODGE ROUSHALL

DANIEL LAINE * MICHAEL WEST * DESIREE MOUZOON PROBLOSKY * TERRI L. WOOD * KAREN WEBBER * PAMELA GRAHAM

JOHNNY BLACKBURN * AUSTIN GALINDO * ALYSSA GALINDO * KILEY GALINDO * KEALA HUGHES * CHRISTINE HISCHAR * THE COMPTON'S * SHELLEY WHITE * SHANNEN SICILIANO * JUSTIN A. BERZON, M.ED. * JODI FECERA * MARY JANE SMITH * MATTHEW SOETH * KELLI R. * BRIAN & NADYA PARTRIDGE

BRIAN W. FREEMAN * ERIN ANDRADE * DR. TRICIA PEÑA * GARY SEGGERMAN * DAVID CANFIELD * DENNIS L. JONES * CANDY LUDEWIG

Add Park on Snapchat
@parksgreatest
www.edalchemy.com

Add Dr. Guy on Snapchat
@guyewhite
www.guyewhite.com

Made in the USA
Coppell, TX
05 December 2022